SIDHE ANCIENT FAERY

MARY ANN BENBOW

Copyright(©)

Mary Ann Benbow reserves the right to this bool. No part of it can be

Reproduced without the written consent of the author.

CONTENT.

Nature of Sidhe.

The Palaces of the Sidhe.

Hill Visions of Sidhe Women.

Minstrels and Music.

The Sidhe as Warriors.

The War Goddess.

The Sidhe in Battle.

The Celtic Faery Faith.

Influence .

The Smallness of Elves.

Under the Shadow of Ben Bulbin.

Evidence .

Irish Mystics .

William Butler Yeats.

Under The Shadow Of Ben Bulbin.

The People of the Goddess Dana, or according to D'Arbois de Jubainville, the People of the god whose mother was called Dana, are the Tuatha De Danann of the ancient mythology of Ireland.

The goddess Dana, called in the genitive Danand, in middle Irish times, was named Bridget. And this goddess Brigit of the pagan Celts has been supplanted by the Christian St. Brigid and, in the same way as the pagan cult once bestowed on the spirits in wells and fountains has been transferred to Christian saints, to whom the wells and fountains have been re-dedicated, so to St. Brigit as a national saint has been transferred the pagan cult rendered to her predecessor. Thus even yet, as in the case of the minor divinities of their sacred fountains, the Irish people, through their veneration for the good St. Brigit, render homage to the divine mother of the people who bear her name Dana—who are the ever-living invisible fairy people of modern Ireland. When the Sons of Mil, the ancestors of the Irish people, came to Ireland, they found the Tuatha de Danann in full possession of the country. The Tuatha De Danann then retired before the invaders, without, however, giving up their sacred island. Assuming invisibility, with the power of any time reappearing in a human-like form before the children of the Sons of Mil, the People of the Goddess Dana became and are the Fairy-Folk, the *Sidhe* of Irish mythology and romance. Therefore it is that today Ireland contains two races—a race visible, which we call Celts, and a race invisible, which we call Fairies. Between these two races there is constant intercourse even now; for Irish seers say that they can behold the majestic, beautiful *Sidhe*, and according to them the *Sidhe* are a race quite distinct from our own, just as living and possibly more powerful. These *Sidhe* (who are the 'gentry' of the BenBulbin country and have kindred elsewhere in Ireland, Scotland,
and probably in most other countries as well, such as the invisible races of the Yosemite Valley) have been described more or less

accurately by our peasant seer-witnesses from County Sligo and North and East Ireland. But there are other and probably more reliable seers in Ireland, men of greater education and greater psychical experience, who know and describe the *Sidhe* races as they really are, and who even sketch their likenesses. And to such seer Celts as these, Death is a passport to the world of the *Sidhe,* a world where there is eternal youth and never-ending joy, as we shall learn when we study it as the Celtic Otherworld.

The recorded mythology and literature of ancient Ireland have, very faithfully for the most part, preserved to us clear pictures of the Tuatha De Danann; so that disregarding some Christian influence in the texts of certain manuscripts, much rationalisation, and a good deal of poetical colouring and romantic imagination in the pictures, we can easily describe the People of the Goddess Dana as they appeared in pagan days, when they were more frequently seen by mortals than now. Perhaps the Irish folk of the olden times were even more clairvoyant and spiritual-minded than the Irish folk of today. So by drawing upon these written records, let us try to understand what sort of beings the *Sidhe* were and are.

NATURE OF THE *SIDE*

In the *Book of Leinster,* the poem of *Eochaid* records that Tuatha De Danann, the conquerors of the Fir-Bolgs, were hosts of *siabra*; and *siabra* is an Old Irish word meaning fairies, sprites, or ghosts. The word fairies is appropriate if restricted to mean fairies like the modern 'gentry'; but the word *ghosts* is inappropriate because our evidence shows that the only relation the *Sidhe* or real fairies hold to ghosts is a superficial one, the *Sidhe* and ghosts being alike only in respect to invisibility. In the two chief Irish MSS., the *Book of the Dun Cow* and the *Book of Leinster*, the Tuatha De Danann are described as 'gods. and not gods; and Sir John Rhy considers this an ancient formula comparable with the Sanskrit *deva* and *a deva*, but not with 'poets (*dée*) and husbandmen (*a dée*),' as the author of *Cóir Anmann* learnedly guessed. It is also said, in the *Book of the Dun Cow*, that wise men do not know the origin of the Tuatha De Danann, but that it seems likely to them that they came from heaven, on account of their intelligence and for the excellence of their knowledge.

The hold of the Tuatha De Danann on the Irish mind and spirit was so strong that even Christian transcribers of texts could not deny their existence as a non-human race of intelligent beings inhabiting Ireland, even though they frequently misrepresented them by placing them on the level of evil demons, as the ending of the story of the *Sick-Bed of Cuchulainn* illustrates: --' So that this was a vision to Cuchulainn of being struck by the people of the *Sid*: for the demoniac power was great before the faith; and such was its greatness that the demons used to fight bodily against mortals, and they used to show them delights and secrets of how they would be in immortality.

It was what they used to believe in. So it is to such phantoms that the ignorant apply the names of *Side* and *Aes Side*.' A passage in the *Silva Gadelica* (ii. 202--3) not only tends to confirm this last statement, but it also shows that the Irish people made a clear distinction between the godrace and our own: --In *The Colloquy with the Ancients*, as St. Patrick and Caeilte are talking with one another, 'a lone woman robbed in mantle of green, a smock of soft silk being next her skin, and on her forehead, a glittering plate of yellow gold,' came to them, and when Patrick asked from whence she came, she replied, 'Out of *uaimh Chruachna*, or "the cave of Cruachan." ' Caeilte then asked, 'Woman, my soul, who art thou?' 'I am *Scothniamh*, or "Flower-lustre," the daughter of the Daghda's son, Bodhb derg.' Camille proceeded: 'And what started thee here?' require thee my marriage gift, because once upon a time thou promisedst me such.' And as they parlayed, Patrick broke in with, 'It is a wonder to us how we see you two: the girl young and invested with all comeliness; but thou Caeilte, a withered ancient, bent in the back and dingily grown grey.' 'Which is no wonder at all,' said Caeilte, 'for no people of one generation or of one time are we: *she is of the Tuatha Dé Danann, who are unfading and whose duration is perennial; I am of the sons of Milesius, that are perishable and fade away.*

The exact distinction is between Caoilte, a withered old--in most ways to be regarded as a ghost called up that Patrick may question him about the history of Ireland--and a fairy woman who is one of

The *Sidhe,* or Tuatha de Danann.

In two of the more ancient Irish texts, the *Echtra Nerai,* or 'Expedition of Nera', a preliminary tale in the introduction to the *Táin bó Cuailnge,* or 'Theft of the Cattle of Cuailnge'; and a passage from the *Togail Bruidne dâ Derga,* or 'Destruction of Da Derga's Hostel', there seems The fairy hosts going into the cave say, 'For the fairy mounds of Erinn are always open about Halloween.' Nera followed after them until he came to their king in a palace of the Tuatha de Danann, seemingly in the cavern or elsewhere underground; where he remained and was married to one of the fairy women. She was who revealed to Nera the secret hiding place, in a mysterious well, of the king's golden crown and then betrayed her.

whole people by reporting to Near the plan they had for attacking Ailill's court on the Halloween to come. Moreover, Nera was permitted by his fairy wife to depart from the *síd,* and he in taking leave of her asked, 'How will it be believed of me that I have gone into the *síd*?' 'Take fruits of summer with you,' said the woman.

Then he took wild garlic with him and primrose and golden fern.' And on the following November Eve, when the *síd* of Cruachan was again open, 'the men of Connaught and the black hosts of exile' under Ailill and Medb plundered it, taking away from it the crown of Bruin out of the well. But 'Nera was left with his people in the *síd,* and has not come out until now, nor will he come till Doom.'

All of this matter is enough in line with the living fairy faith: there is the same belief expressed as now about November Eve being the time of all times when ghosts, demons, spirits, and fairies are free, and when fairies *take* mortals and marry them to fairy women; also the beliefs that fairies are living in secret places in hills, in caverns, or underground--palaces full of treasure and open only on November Eve. In so far as the real fairies, the *Sidhe*, are concerned, they appear as the rulers of the Feast of the Dead or *Samain*, as the controllers of all spirits who are then at large; and, allowing for some poetical imagination and much social psychology and anthropomorphism, elements as common in this as in most literary descriptions concerning the Tuatha de Danann, they are faithfully enough presented.
.
The second text describes how King Conaire, in riding along a road toward Tara, saw in front of him three strange horsemen, three men of the *Sidhe:* --'Three red frocks had they, and three red mantles: three red steeds they bestrode, and three red heads of hair were on them. Red were they all, both body and hair and raiment, both steeds and men.' 'Who is it that fares before us?' asked Conaire. 'It was a taboo of mine for those three to go before me--the three Reds—to the house of Red. Who will follow them and tell them to come towards me in my tracks?' 'I will follow.
them,' says Léfri Flaith, Conaire's son. 'He goes after them, lashing his horse, and overtaking them not. There was the length of a spearcast between them: but they did not gain upon him, and he did not gain upon them.' All attempts to come up with the red horsemen failed. But at last, before they disappeared, one of the Three said to the king's son riding so furiously behind them, 'Lo, my son, greet the news. Weary are the horses we ride. We ride the steeds of Donn Tetscorach (?) from the elfmounds. Though we are alive, are dead alive, are they? the destruction of life: saying of ravens: fe; ding of crows, the strife of

slaughter: wetting of sword edges, shedgesordedges; okayen bosses in hours after sundown. Lo, my son!' Then they disappear. When Conaire and his followers heard the message, fear fell upon them, and the king said: 'All my taboos have seized me tonight, since those Three [Reds] [are the] banished folks (?).' In this passage, we behold three horsemen of the *Sidhe* banished from their elf mound because they were guilty of falsehood. Visible for a time, they precede the king and so violate one of his taboos; and then delivering their fearful prophecy they vanish. These three of the Tuatha De Danann, majestic and powerful and weird in their mystic red, are like the warriors of the 'gentry' seen by contemporary seers in West Ireland.

Though dead, that is in an invisible world like the dead, yet they are living. It seems that in all three of the textual examples already cited, the scribe has emphasised a different element in the unique nature of the Tuatha De Danann. In the *Colloquy* it is their eternal youth and beauty, in the *Echtra Nerai* it is their supremacy over ghosts and demons on *Samain* and their power to steal mortals away at such a time, and in this last their respect for honesty. And in each case, their portrayal corresponds to that of the 'gentry' and *Sidhe* by modern Irishmen; so that the old Fairy Faith and the new combine to prove the People of the God whose mother was Dana to have been and to be a race of beings who are like mortals, but not mortals, who to the objective world are as though dead, yet to the subjective world are fully living and conscious.

O'Curry says:--'The term (*sídh*, pron. *shee*), as far as we know it, is always applied in old writings to the palaces, courts, halls, or residences of those beings which in ancient Gaedhelic mythology held the place which ghosts, phantoms, and fairies hold in the superstitions of the present day.' In modern Irish tradition, 'the People of the *Sidhe*,' or simply the *Sidhe*, refer to the beings themselves rather than to their places of habitation. Partly perhaps on account of this popular opinion that the *Sidhe* are a subterranean race, they are sometimes described as gods of the earth or *dei terreni*, as in the *Book of Armagh*; and since it was believed that they, like the modern fairies, control the ripening of crops and the milk-giving of cows, the ancient Irish rendered to them regular worship and sacrifice, just as the Irish of to-day do by setting out food at night for the fairy-folk to eat.

Thus after their conquest, these *Sidhe* or Tuatha De Danann in retaliation, and perhaps to show their power as agricultural gods, destroyed the wheat and milk of their conquerors, the Sons of Mil, as fairies today can do; and the Sons of Mil were constrained to make a treaty with their supreme king, Dagda, who, in *Cóir Anman*, is himself called an earth-god. Then when the treaty was made the Sons of Mil were once more able to gather wheat in their fields and to drink the milk of their cows; [2] and we can suppose that ever since that time their descendants, who are the people of Ireland, remembering that treaty, have continued to reverence the People of the Goddess Dana by pouring libations of milk to them and by making them offerings of the fruits of the earth.

THE PALACES OF THE *SIDHE*
The marvellous palaces to which the Tuatha De Danann retired when conquered by the race of Mil were hidden in
the depths of the earth, in hills, or under ridges more or less elevated. At the time of their conquest, Dagda, their high king, made a distribution of all such palaces in his kingdom. He gave one *síd* to Lug, son of Ethne, another to Ogme, and for himself retained two--one called *Brug na Boinne*, or Castle of the Boyne, because it was situated on or near the River Boyne near Tara, and the other called *Síd* or *Brug Magic in Oc*, which means Enchanted Palace or Castle of the Son of the Young. And this Mac and Oc was Dagda's son by the queen

Boann, according to some accounts, so that as the name (Son of the Young) signifies, Dagda and Boann, both immortals, both Tuatha De Danann, were necessarily always young, never knowing the touch of disease, decay, or old age. Not until Christianity gained its psychic triumph at Tara, through the magic of Patrick prevailing against the magic of the Druids--who seem to have stood at that time as mediators between the People of the Goddess Dana and the pagan Irish--did the Tuatha De Danann lose their immortal youthfulness in the eyes of mortals and become subject to death. In the most ancient manuscripts of Ireland, the pre-Christian doctrine of the immortality of the divine race 'persisted intact and without restraint, but in the *Senchus na relic,* or 'History of the Cemeteries', from the *Leabhar na h-Uidhir*, and in the *Lebar gable,* or 'Book of the Conquests', from the *Book of Leinster*, it was completely changed by the Christian scribes.

When Dagda thus distributed the underground palaces, Mac and Oc, or as he was otherwise called Oengus, was absent and hence forgotten. So when he returned, naturally he complained to his father, and the *Brug na Boinne,* the king's residence, was ceded to him for a night and a day, but Oengus maintained that it was forever. This palace was a most marvellous one: it contained three trees which always bore fruit, a vessel full of excellent drink, and two pigs--one alive and the other nicely cooked ready to eat
at any time; and in this palace, no one ever died.
In the *Colloquy*, Caeilte tells of a mountain containing a fairy palace in which no man saved Finn and six companions, Caeilte being one of these, ever entered.
The Fenians, while hunting, were led thither by a fairy woman who had changed her shape to that of a fawn to lure them; and the night being wild and snowy they were glad to take shelter in.

Beautiful damsels and their lovers were the inhabitants of the palace; in it, there was music and an abundance of food and drink; and on its floor stood a chair of crystal.

In another fairy palace, the enchanted cave of Keshcorran, Conran, son of Model, chief of the Tuatha De Danann, had sway; 'and so soon as he perceived that the hounds' cry now sounded devious, he bade his three daughters (that were full of sorcery) to go and take vengeance on Finn for his hunting ' ust as nowadays the 'good people' take vengeance on one of our race if a fairy domain is violated. Frequently the fairy palace is under a lake, as in the Christianised story of the *Disappearance of Caenchomrac*:--Once when 'the cleric chanted his psalms, he saw [come] towards him a tall man that emerged out of the loch: from the bottom of 'the water that is to say.' This tall man informed the cleric that he came from an underwater monastery, and explained 'that there should be subaqueous inhabiting by men is with God no harder than that they should dwell in any other place'.In all these ancient literary accounts of the Sidhe-palaces, we easily recognize the same sort of palaces as those described today by Gaelic peasants as the habitations of the gentry', or 'good people', or 'people of peace.' Such habitations are in mountain caverns like those of Ben Bulbin or Knock Ma, or fairy hills or knolls like the Fairy Hill at Aberfoyle on which Robert Kirk is believed to have been *taken*, or beneath lakes. This brings us directly to how the *Sidhe* or Tuatha De Danann of the olden times *took* fine-looking young men and maidens.

HOW THE *SIDHE* 'TOOK' MORTALS

Perhaps one of the earliest and most famous literary accounts of such a *taking* is that concerning Aedh, son of Eochaid Lethderg son of 'the King of Leinster, who is represented as contemporary with Patrick. While Aedh was enjoying a game of hurley with his boy companions near the *sidh* of Liamhain Softsmock, two of the *sidh*-women, who

loved the young prince, very suddenly appeared, and as suddenly took him away with them into a fairy palace and kept him there three years. It happened, however, that he escaped at the end of that time, and, knowing the magical powers of Patrick, went to where the holy man was, and thus explained himself:Against the youths my opponents I (i.e. my side) took seven goals; but at the last one that I took, here come up to me two women clad in green mantles: two daughters of *Bodb derg mac a Daghda*, and their names *Slad* and *Mumain*. Either of them took me by a hand, and they led me off to a garish *brugh*; whereby for now three years my people mourn after me, the *sídh*-folk caring for me ever since, and until last night I got a chance opening to escape from the *brugh*, when to the number of fifty lads we emerged out of the *sídh* and forth upon the green. Then it was that I considered the magnitude of that strait in which they of the *sídh* had had me, and away from the *Brugh* I came running to seek you, holy Patrick.' 'That,' said the saint, 'shall be to a safeguard, so that neither their power nor their dominion shall any more prevail against you..' And so when Patrick had thus made Aedh proof against the power of the fairy-folk, he kept him with him under the disguise of a travelling minstrel until, arriving in Leinster, he restored him to his father the king and his inheritance: Aedh enters the palace in his minstrel disguise; and in the presence of the royal assembly Patrick commands him: 'Doff now once for all thy dark capacious hood, and well mayest thou wear thy father's spear!' When the lad removed his hood, and none there but recognized him, grea
was the surprise. He seemed like one came back from the dead, for long had his heirless father and people mourned for him. 'By our word,' exclaimed the assembly in their joyous excitement, 'it is a good cleric's gift!' And the king said: 'Holy Patrick, seeing that till this day thou hast nourished him and nurtured, let not the Tuatha De Danann's power any more prevail against the lad.' And Patrick answered: 'That death which the King of Heaven and Earth hath ordained is the one

that he will have.' This ancient legend shows clearly that the Tuatha De Danann, or *Sidhe*, in the time when the scribe wrote the *Colloquy* were thought of in the same way as now, as able to *take* beautiful mortals whom they loved, and able to confer upon them fairy immortality which prevented 'that death which the King of Heaven and Earth hath ordained'.

Mortals did it, could live in the world of the *Sidhe* forever, and we shall see this more fully in our study of the Otherworld. But here it will be interesting to learn that, unlike Aedh, whom some perhaps would call a foolish youth, Laeghaire, also a prince, for he was the son of the king of Connaught, entered a *dun* of the *Sidhe*, taking fifty other warriors with him; and he and his followers found life in Fairyland so pleasant that they all decided to enjoy it eternally. Accordingly, when they had been there a year, they planned to return to Connaught to bid the king and his people a final farewell. They announced their plan, and Fiachna of the *Sidhe* told them how to accomplish it safely:--' If ye would come back take with your horses, but by no means dismount from off them'; 'So it was done: they went their way and came upon a general assembly in which Connaught, as at the year expired, mourned for the aforesaid warrior-band, whom now all at once they perceived above them (i. e. on higher ground). Connaught sprang to meet them, but Laoghaire cried: "Approach us not [to touch us]: 'tis to bid you farewell that we are here!" "Leave me not!" Crimthann, his father, said: "Connaught's royal power be thine; their silver and their gold, their horses with their bridles, and their
noblewomen be at thy discretion, only leave me not!" But Laoghaire turned from them and so entered again into the *sídh*, where with Fiachna he exercises joint kingly rule; nor has he as yet come out of it.'

HILL VISIONS OF *SIDHE* WOMEN

There are many recorded traditions which represent certain hills as mystical places where men are favoured with visions of fairy women. Thus, one day King Muirchertach came forth to hunt on the border of the Brugh (near Stackallen Bridge, County Meath), and his companions left him alone on his hunting mound. 'He had not been there long when he saw a solitary damsel beautifully formed, fair-haired, bright-skinned, with a green mantle about her sitting near him on the turf mound; and it seemed to him that of womankind he had never beheld her equal in beauty and refinement.' [1] In the Mabinogi of *Pwyll, Prince of Duvet*, which seems to be only a Brythonic treatment of an original Gaelic tale, Pwyll seating himself on a mound where any mortal sitting might see a prodigy, saw a fairy woman ride past on a white horse, and she clad in a garment of shining gold. Though he tried to have his servitor on the swiftest horse capture her, 'There was some magic about the lady that kept her always the same distance ahead, though she appeared to be riding slowly.' When on the second day Pwyll returned to the mound the fairy woman came riding by as before, and the servitor again gave an unsuccessful chase. Pwyll saw her in the same manner on the third day. He then gave chase himself, and when he exclaimed to her, 'For the sake of the man whom you love, wait for me!' she stopped; and by mutual arrangement, the two agreed to meet and to marry at the end of a year.

THE MINSTRELS OR MUSICIANS OF THE *SIDHE*

Not only did the fairy folk of more ancient tunes enjoy wonderful places full of beauty and riches, and a life of eternal youth, but they also had, even as now, minstrelsy and rare music--music to which that of our world could not be compared at all; for even Patrick himself said that it would equal the very music of heaven if it were not for a twang of the fairy spell that infests it. [3] And this is how it was that Patrick heard the fairy music:--As he was travelling through Ireland he once sat down on a grassy knoll, as he often did in the good old Irish way, with Ulidia's king and nobles and Castle also: 'Nor were they long there before they saw draw near them a *scológ* or "non-warrior" that wore a fair green mantle having in it a fibula of silver; a shirt of yellow silk next his skin, over and outside that again a tunic of soft satin, and with a *timpán* (a sort of harp) of the best slung on his back. "Whence comest thou, *scológ*?"--asked the king. "Out of the *sídh* of the Daghda's son Bodhb Derg, out of Ireland's southern part." "What moved thee out of the south, and who art thou thyself?" "I am Cascorach, son of Cainchinn who is an ollave to the Tuatha De Danann and am myself the makings of an *ollave* (i.e. an aspirant to the grade). What started me was the design to acquire knowledge, information, and lore for a recital, and Fianna's mighty deeds of valour, from Caeilte son of Ronan." Then he took his *timpán* and made for them music and minstrelsy so that he sent them slumbering off to sleep.' And Cascorach's music was pleasing to Patrick, who said of it: 'Good indeed it was, but for a twang of the fairy spell that infests it; barring which nothing could more nearly resemble Heaven's harmony.' [1] And that very night which followed the day on which the *ollave* to the Tuatha De Danann came to them was the Eve of *Samhain*. There was also another of these fairy *timpán*-players called 'the wondrous elfin man', 'Aillén mac Midhna of the Tuatha De Danann, that out of *sídh* Donnchaidh to the northward used to come to Tara: the manner of his coming being with a musical *timpán* in his hand, the which whenever any heard he would at once sleep. Then, all being lulled thus, out of his mouth Aillén would emit a blast of fire. It was on the solemn *Samhain Day* (November Day) that he came in every year, played his *timpán*, and to the fairy music that he made all hands would fall asleep. With his breath, he used to blow up the flame and so, during a three-and-twenty years' spell, yearly burnt up Tara with all her gear.' And it is said that Finn, finally overcoming the magic of Aillén, slew him. [1]

Perhaps in the first musician, Cascorach, though he is described as the son of a Tuatha De Danann minstrel, we behold a mortal like one of the many Irish pipers and musicians who used to go, or even go yet, to the fairy-folk to be educated in the musical profession, and then come back as the most marvellous players that ever were in Ireland; though if Cascorach were once a mortal it seems that he has been quite transformed in bodily nature to be one of the Tuatha De Danann himself. But Allen mac Midhna is undoubtedly one of the mighty 'gentry' who could--as we heard from County Sligo--destroy half the human race if they wished. Aillén visits Tara, the old psychic centre both for Ireland's high-kings and its Druids. He comes as it were against the conquerors of his race, who in their neglectfulness no longer render due worship and sacrifice on the Feast of *Samhain* to the Tuatha De Danann, the gods of 'the dead, at that time supreme; and then it is that he works his magic against the royal palaces of the kings and Druids on the ancient Hill. And to overcome the magic of Aillén and slay him, that is, make it impossible for him to repeat his annual visits to Tara, it required the might of the great hero Finn, who himself was related to the same *Sidhe* race, for by a woman of the Tuatha De Danann he had his famous son Ossian (Oisin).

In *Gilla dé*, who is Manannan mac Lir, the greatest magician of the Tuatha De Danann, disguised as a being who can disappear in the twinkling of an eye whenever he wishes, and reappear unexpectedly as a 'kern that wore the garb of yellow stripes', we meet with another fairy musician. And to him, O'Donnell says:--' By Heaven's grace again, since first I heard the fame of them that within the hills and under the earth beneath us make the fairy music,. . . music sweeter than thy strains I have never heard; thou art in sooth a most melodious rogue!' [2] And again it is said of him:--' Then the *gilla decair* taking a harp played music so sweet. . . and the king after a momentary glance at his musicians never knew which way he went from him.'

SOCIAL ORGANISATION AND WARFARE AMONG THE *SIDE*

So far, we have seen only the happy side of the life of the Sidhe-folk--their palaces and pleasures and music; but there was a more human (or anthropomorphic) side to their nature in which they wage war on one another, and have their matrimonial troubles even as we moderns. And we turn now to examine this other side of their life, to behold the *Sidhe* as a warlike race; and as we do so let us remember that the 'gentry' in the BenBulbin country and all Ireland, and the people of Finvara in Knock Ma, and also the invisible races of California, are likewise described as given to war and mighty feats of arms.

The invisible Irish races have always had a very distinct social organisation, so distinct in fact that Ireland can be divided according to its fairy kings and fairy queens and their territories even now; and no doubt we see in this how the ancient Irish anthropomorphically projected into an animistic belief their social conditions and racial characteristics. This social organisation and territorial division ought to be understood before we discuss the social troubles and consequent wars of the *Sidhe*-folk. For example in Munster Bodb was king and his enchanted palace was called the *Síd* of the Men of Femen, and we already know about the over-king Dagda and his Boyne palace near Tara. In more modern times, especially in popular fairy traditions, Evil or Eevinn (*Aoibhill* or *Aolbhinn*) of the *Craig Liath* or Grey Rock is a queen of the Munster fairies; and Finvarra is the king of the Connaught fairies

Irish fairy queens

We are now prepared to see the Tuatha De Danann in their domestic troubles and wars; and the following story is as interesting as any, for in it Dagda himself is the chief actor. Once when his son Oengus fell sick of a love sickness, King Dagda, who ruled all the *Sidhe*-folk in Ireland, joined forces with Ailill and Medb to compel Ethel Annual to deliver up his beautiful daughter Caer whom Oengus loved. When Ethyl Anbual's palace had been stormed and Ethal Annual reduced to submission, he declared he had no power over his daughter Caer, for on the first of November each year, he said, she changed to a swan, or from a swan to a maiden again. 'The first of November next,' he added, 'my daughter will be under the form of a swan, near the Loch bel Draccon. Marvellous birds will be seen there: my daughter will be surrounded by a hundred and fifty other swans.'

When the November Day arrived, Oengus went to the lake, and, seeing the swans and recognizing Caer, plunged into the water and instantly became a swan with her. While under the form of swans, Oengus and Caer went together to the Boyne palace of the king Dagda, his father, and remained there; and their singing was so sweet that all who heard it slept three days and three nights. [1] In this story, new elements like the *Sidhe* appear, though like modern ones: the *Sidhe* can assume other forms than their own, are subject to enchantments like mortals; and when under the form of swans are in some perhaps superficial aspects like the swan-maidens in stories which are world-wide, and their swan-song has the same sweetness and magical effect as in other countries In the Rennes *Dindshenchas* there is a tale about a war among the 'men of the Elfmounds' over 'two lovable maidens who dwelt in the elf mound', and when they delivered the battle 'they all shaped themselves into the

shapes of deer Midir's Sons under Donn mac Midir, in rebellion against the Daghda's son Bodh Derg, fled away to an obscure *sídh*, where in yearly battle they met the hosts of the other Tuatha De Danann under Bodh Derg; and it was into this *sídh* or fairy palace on the very eve before the annual contest that Finn and his six companions were enticed by the fairy woman in the form of a fawn, to secure their aid. And in another tale, Laeghaire, son of the king of Connaught, with fifty warriors, plunged into a lake to the fairy world beneath it, to assist the fairy man, who came thence to them, to recover his wife stolen by a rival.

THE *SIDHE* AS WAR GODDESSES OR THE *BADB*

It is in the form of birds that certain of the Tuatha De Danann appear as war goddesses and directors of battle,-and we learn from one of our witnesses that the 'gentry' or modern *Sidhe*-folk take sides even now in a great war, like that between Japan and Russia. It is in their relation to the hero Cuchulainn that one can best study the People of the Goddess Dana in their role as controllers of human war. In the greatest of the Irish epics, the *Tam Bó Cuailnge*, where Cuchulainn is under their influence, these war goddesses are called *Badb* (or *Bodb*) which here seems to be a collective term for *Neman*, *Macha*, and *Morrigu* (or *Morrigan*)--each of whom exercises a particular supernatural power. *Neman* appears as the confounder of armies, so that friendly bands, bereft of their senses by her, slaughter one another; *Macha* is a fury that riots and rebels among the slain; while *Morrigu*, the greatest of the three, by her presence infuses superhuman valour into Cuchulainn, nerves him for the cast, and guides the course of his unerring spear. And the Tuatha De Danann in infusing this valour into the great hero show themselves--as we already know them to be on *Samhain* Eve--the rulers of all sorts of demons of the air and awful spirits:--In the *Book of Leinster* (fol. 57, B 2) it is recorded that 'the satyrs, and sprites, and maniacs of the valleys, and demons of the air, shouted about him, for the Tuatha De Danann were wont to impart their valour to him, so that he might be more feared, more dreaded, more terrible, in every battle and battle-field, in every combat and conflict, into which he went.'

The Battles of Moytura seem in most ways to be nothing more than the traditional record of long warfare to determine the future spiritual control of Ireland, carried on between two opposed orders of invisible beings, the Tuatha De Danann representing the gods of light and good and the Fomorians representing the gods of darkness and evil. It is said that after the second of these battles 'The *Morrigu*, daughter of Ermas (the Irish war-goddess), proceeded to proclaim that battle and the mighty victory which had taken place, to the royal heights of Ireland and its fairy host and its chief waters and its river-mouths '.For good had prevailed over evil, and it was settled that all Ireland should forever afterwards be a sacred country ruled over by the People of the Goddess Dana and the Sons of Mil jointly. So here we see the Tuatha De Danann with their war goddess fighting their own battles in which human beings play no part.

It is interesting to observe that this Irish war-goddess, the *body* or *bad*, considered of old to be one of the Tuatha De Danann, has survived to our day in the fairy lore of the chief Celtic countries. In Ireland, survival is best seen in the popular and still almost general belief among the peasantry that the fairies often exercise their magical powers under the form of Royston crows; and for this

These birds are always greatly dreaded and avoided. The resting of one of them on a peasant's cottage may signify many things, but often it means the death of one of the family or some great misfortune, the bird in such a case playing the part of a *bean-sidhe* (banshee). And this folk belief finds its echo in the recorded tales of Wales, Scotland, and Brittany. In the *Mabinogi*, 'Dream of Rhonabwy,' Owain, prince of Rheged and a contemporary of Arthur, has a wonderful crow which always secures his victory in battle with the aid of three hundred other crows under its leadership. In Campbell's *Popular Tales of the West Highlands*, the fairies very often exercise their power in the form of the common hooded crow, and in Brittany, there is a folk tale entitled '*Les Compagnons*' [1] in which the chief actor is a fairy under the form of a magpie who lives in a royal forest just outside Rennes

W. M. Hennessy has shown that the word *body* or *bad*, aspirated *bodhbh* or *badhbh* (pronounced *bov* or *bad*), originally signified rage, fury, or violence, and ultimately implied a witch, fairy, or goddess; and that as the memory of this Irish goddess of war survives in folk-lore, her emblem is the well-known scald-crow, or Royston-crow. [3] By referring to Peter O'Connell's *Irish Dictionary* we can confirm this popular belief which identifies the battle fairies with the Royston-crow, and discover that there is a definite relationship or even identification between the *Badb* and the *Bean-sidhe* or banshee, as there is in modern Irish folklore between the Royston-crow and the fairy who announces a death. *Badb-catha* is made to equal 'Fionog, a Royston-crow, a squall crow'; *Badb* is defined as a '*bean-sidhe*, a female fairy, phantom, or spectre, supposed to be attached to certain families, and to appear sometimes in the form of squall-crows, or Royston-crows'; and the *Badb* in the threefold aspect is thus explained: '*Macha,* i. e. a Royston-crow; *Morrighan*, i. e. the great fairy; *Neamhan*, i. e. *Badb Catha no feeling*; *a bad Catha*, or Royston-crow.' Similar explanations are given by other glossarists, and thus the evidence of etymological scholarship as well as that of folk-lore support the Psychological Theory.

THE *SIDHE* IN THE BATTLE OF CLONTARF, A. D. 1014
The People of the Goddess Dana played an important part in human warfare even so late as the Battle of Clontarf, fought near Dublin, on April 23, 1014; and at that time fairy women and phantom-hosts were to the Irish unquestionable existences, as real as ordinary men and women. It is recorded in the manuscript story of the battle, of which numerous copies exist, that the fairy woman Aoibheall [1] came to Dunlang O'Hartigan before the battle and begged him not to fight, promising him life and happiness for two hundred years if he would put off fighting for a single day; but the patriotic Irishman expressed his decision to fight for Ireland, and then the fairy woman foretold how he and his friend Murrough, and Brian and Conaing and all the nobles of Erin and even his son Turlough, were fated to fall in the conflict.

On the eve of the battle, Dunlang comes to his friend Murrough directly from the fairy woman; and Murrough upon seeing him reproaches him for his absence in these -words:--'Great must be the love and attachment of some woman for thee which has induced thee to abandon me.' 'Alas O King,' answered Dunlang, 'the delight which I have abandoned for thee is greater if thou didst but know it, namely, life without death, without cold, without thirst, without hunger, without decay, beyond any delight of the delights of the earth to me, until the judgement, and heaven after the judgement; and if I had not pledged my word to thee I would not have come here; moreover, it is fated for me to die on the day that thou shalt die.' When Murrough has heard this terrible message, the prophecy of his death in the battle, despondency seizes him; and then it is that he declares that he for Ireland like Dunlang for honour has also sacrificed the opportunity of entering and living in that wonderful Land of Eternal Youth:--' Often was I offered in hills, and fairy mansions, this world (the fairy world) and these gifts, but I never abandoned for one night my country nor mine inheritance for them.'

And thus is described the meeting of the two armies at Clontarf, and the demons of the air and the phantoms, and all the hosts of the invisible world who were assembled to scatter confusion and to revel in the bloodshed, and how above them in supremacy rose the *Badb*:--' It will be one of the wonders of the day of judgement to relate the description of this tremendous onset. There arose a wild, impetuous, precipitate, mad, inexorable, furious, dark, lacerating, merciless, combative, contentious *bad*, which was shrieking and fluttering over their heads. And there arose also the satyrs, and sprites, and the maniacs of the valleys, and the witches, and goblins, and owls, and destroying demons of the air and sky, and the demoniac phantom host, and they were inciting and sustaining valour and battle with

them.'It is said of Murrough (*Murchadh*) as he entered the thick of the fight and prepared to assail the
foreign invaders, the Danes when they had repulsed the Dal-Cais, that 'he was seized with boiling terrible anger, an excessive elevation and greatness of spirit and mind. A bird of valour and championship rose in him and fluttered over his head and on his breath

CONCLUSION

The recorded or manuscript Fairy-Faith of the Gaels corresponds in all essentials with the living Gaelic Fairy-Faith: the Tuatha De Danann or *Sidhe*, the 'Gentry', the 'Good People', and the 'People of Peace' are described as a race of invisible divine beings eternally young and unfading. They inhabit fairy palaces, enjoy rare feasts and love-making, and have their music and minstrelsy. They are essentially majestic; they wage war in their invisible realm against other of its inhabitants like the ancient Fomorians; they frequently direct human warfare or nerve the arm of a great hero like Cuchulainn; and demons of the air, spirit hosts, and awful unseen creatures obey them. Mythologically they are gods of light and good, able to control natural phenomena to make harvests come forth abundantly or not at all. But they are not such mythological beings as we read about in scholarly dissertations on mythology, dissertations so learned in their curious and unreasonable and often unintelligible hypotheses about the workings of the mind among primitive men. How social psychology has deeply affected all such animistic beliefs was pointed out above in chapter iii. In chapter xi, entitled *Science and Fairies*, our position concerning the essential nature of the fairy races will be made clear.

THE CELTIC FAIRY FAITH IS PART OF A WORLDWIDE ANIMISM

The modern belief in fairies, with which until now we have been specifically concerned, is Celtic only in so far as it reflects Celtic traditions and customs, Celtic myth and religion, and Celtic social and environmental conditions. Otherwise, as will be shown throughout this and succeeding chapters, it is, in essence, a part of worldwide

animism, which forms the background of all religions in whatever stage of culture religions exist or to which they have attained by evolution, from the barbarism of the Congo black man to the civilization of the Archbishop of Canterbury; and as far back as we can go into human origins there is some corresponding belief in a fairy or spirit realm, as there is to-day among contemporary civilised and uncivilised races of all countries. We may therefore very profitably begin
our examination of the living Fairy-Faith of the Celts by comparing it with a few examples, taken almost at random, from the animistic beliefs current among non-Celtic peoples.
To the Arunta tribes of Central Australia, furthest removed in space from the Celts and hence least likely to have been influenced by them, let us go first, to examine their doctrine of ancestral *Alcheringa* beings and of the *Iruntarinia*, which offers an almost complete parallel to the Celtic belief in fairies. These *Alcheringa* beings and *Iruntarinia*--to ignore the secondary differences between the two--are a spirit race inhabiting an invisible or fairy world. Only certain persons, medicine men and seers, can see them; and these describe them as thin and shadowy, and, like the Irish *Sidhe*, as always youthful in appearance. Precisely like their Celtic counterparts in general, these Australian spirits are believed to haunt inanimate objects such as stones and trees; or to frequent totem centres, as in Ireland demons (daemons) are believed to frequent certain places known to have been anciently dedicated to the religious rites of the pre-Christian Celts; and, quite after the manner of the Breton dead and of most fairies, they are said to control human affairs and natural phenomena. All the Arunta invariably regard themselves as incarnations or reincarnations of these ancestral spirit-beings; and, by evidence to be outlined in our seventh chapter, ancient and modern Celts have likewise regarded themselves as incarnations or reincarnations of ancestors and of fairy beings. Also, the Arunta think of the *Alcheringa* beings exactly as

Celts think of fairies: as real invisible entities who must be propitiated if men wish to secure their goodwill; and as beneficent and protecting beings when not offended, who may attach themselves to individuals as guardians spirits among the Melanesian peoples there is an equally firm faith in spiritual beings, which they call *Vui* and *Wui*, and these beings have very many of the chief attributes of the *Alcheringa* being Africa, the *Amatongo*, or *Abapansi* of Amazulu belief, have essentially the same motives for action toward men and women, and exhibit the same powers, as the Scotch and Irish peasants assign to the 'good people'. They *take* the living through death; and people so *taken* appear afterwards as apparitions, having become *Amatongo*. In the New World, we find in the North American Red Men a race as much given as the Celts are to a belief in various spirits like fairies. They believe that there are spirits in lakes, rivers and waterfalls, in rocks and trees, in the earth and the air; and that these beings produce storms, droughts, good and bad harvests, abundance and scarcity of game, disease, and the varying fortunes of men. Mr. Leland, who has carefully studied these American beliefs, says that the *Un à games-suk*, or little spirits inhabiting rocks and streams, play a much more influential part in the social and religious life of the North American Red Men than elves or fairies ever did among the Aryans. In Asia, there is the well-known and elaborate animistic creed of the Chinese and the Japanese, to be in part illustrated in subsequent sections. In popular Indian belief, as found in the Punjab, there is no essential difference between various orders of beings endowed with immortality, such as ghosts and spirits on the one hand, and gods, demigods, and warriors on the other; for whether in bodies in this world or out of bodies in the invisible world, they equally live and act--quite as fairies do. Throughout the Malay Peninsula, belief in many orders of good and bad spirits, demon possession, exorcism, and the power of black magicians is very common. But in the *Phi* races of Siam,

we discover what is probably the most important and complete parallel to the Celtic Fairy Faith existing in Asia.
According to the Siamese folk belief, all the stars and various planets, as well as the ethereal spaces, are the dwelling places of the *Thévadas*, gods and goddesses of the old pre-Buddhist mythology, who correspond pretty closely to the Tuatha De Danann of Irish mythology; and this world itself is peopled by legions of minor deities called *Phi*, who include all the various orders of good and bad spirits continually influencing mankind. Some of these *Phi* live in forests, in trees, in open spaces; and watercourses are full of them. Others inhabit mountains and high places. A particular order that haunts the sacred trees surrounding the Buddhist temples is known as *Phi nang mai*; and since *nang* is the word for female, and *mai* for the tree, they are comparable to tree-dwelling fairies, or Greek wood-nymphs. Still another order called *Chau phi phi* (gods of the earth) are like house-frequenting brownies, fairies, and pixies, or like certain orders of *Corrigan's* who haunt barns, stables, and dwellings; and in many curious details, these *Chao phum phi* correspond to the Penates of ancient Rome.
Not only is the worship of this order of *Phi* widespread in Siam, but in every other order of *Phi* altars are erected and propitiatory offerings made by all classes of the Siamese people. Before passing westwards to Europe, in completion of our rapid folk-lore tour of the world, we may observe that the Persians, even those who are well educated, have a firm belief in *jinns* and *afores*, different orders of good and bad spirits with all the chief characteristics of fairies. Modern Arabs Egyptians and Egyptian Turks hold similar animistic beliefs.
In Europe, the Greek peasant as firmly believes in nymphs or nereids as the Celtic peasant believes in fairies; and nymphs, nereids, and fairies alike are often the survivors of ancient mythology. Mr J. C. Lawson, who has very carefully investigated the folk-lore of modern Greece, says: 'The nereids are conceived as women half-divine yet

not immortal, always young, always beautiful, capricious at best, and at their worst cruel. Their presence is suspected everywhere. I had a nerd pointed out to me by my guide, and there certainly was the semblance of a female figure draped in white, and tall beyond human stature, flitting in the dusk between the gnarled and twisted boles of an old olive yard. What the apparition was, I had no leisure to investigate; for my guide with many signs of the cross and muttered invocations of the Virgin urged my mule to perilous haste along the rough mountain path.' Like Celtic fairies, these Greek nereids have their queens; they dance all night, disappearing at cock-crow; they can cast spells on animals or maladies on men and women; they can shift their shape; they *take* children in death and make changelings; and they fall in love with young men.

Among the Roumain peoples, the widespread belief in the *lele* shows in other ways equally marked parallels with the Fairy Faith of the Celts. These *lele* wait at crossroads and near dwellings, or at village fountains or in fields and woods, where they can best cast on men and women various maladies. Sometimes they fall in love with beautiful young men and women and have on such occasions even been controlled by their mortal lovers. They are extremely fond of music and dancing, and many a shepherd with his pipes has been favoured by them, though they have their music and songs too. The Albanian peoples have evil fairies, no taller than children twelve years old, called in Modern Greek τὰ ἐξωτικά, 'those without,' who correspond to the *lele*. Young people who have been enticed to enter their round dance afterwards waste away and die, apparently becoming one of 'those without'. These Albanian spirits, like the 'good people' and the Breton dead, have their particular paths and retreats, and whoever violates these is struck and falls ill. These parallels from Roumain lands are probably due to the close Aryan relationship between the Roumains, the Greeks, and the Celts. The *lele* seem nothing more than the nymphs and nereids of classical antiquity transformed under Christian influence into beings who contradict their original good character, as in Celtic lands the fairy-folk have likewise come to be fallen angels and evil spirits. There is an even closer relationship between the Italian and Celtic fairies. For example, among the Etruscan-Roman people there are now flourishing animistic beliefs almost identical in all details to the Fairy Faith of the Celts. In a very valuable study on Neo-Latin Fay, Mr. H. C. Coote writes:--' Who were the Days--the *fate* of later Italy, the *fées* of mediaeval France? For it is clear that the *fatua*, *fata*, and *fée* are all the same word.' He proceeds to show that the race of immortal damsels whom the old natives of Italy called *Father* gave origin to all the family of *fées* as these appear in Latin countries and that the Italians recognized in the Greek nymphs their *Fate*. It is quite evident that we have here discovered in Italy, as we discovered in Greece and Roumain lands, fairies very Celtic in character; and should further examination be made of modern European folk-lore yet other similar fairies would be found, such, for example, as the elves of Germany and Scandinavia, or as the *servants* of the Swiss peasant. And in all cases, whether the beliefs examined be Celtic or non-Celtic, Aryan or non-Aryan, from Australia, Polynesia, Africa, America, Asia, or Europe, they are in essence animalistically the same, as later sections in this chapter will make clear. But while the parallelism of these beliefs is indicated it is, of course, not meant for a moment that in all of the cases or any one of the cases the specific differences are not considerable. The ground of comparison consists simply of those generic characteristics which these fairy faiths, as they may be called, invariably display--characteristics which we have good precedent for summing up in the single adjective animistic.

SHAPING INFLUENCE OF SOCIAL PSYCHOLOGY
For the term animism, we have to thank Dr. E. B. Tylor, whose *Primitive Culture*, in which the animistic theory is developed, may

almost be said to mark the beginning of scientific anthropology. In this work, however, there is a decided tendency (which indeed displays itself in most of the leading anthropological works, as, for example, in those by Dr Frazer) to regard men, or at any rate primitive men, as having a mind homogeneous, and therefore as thinking, feeling, and acting in the same way under all conditions alike. But a decided change is beginning to manifest itself in the interpretation of the customs and beliefs of the ruder races. It is assumed as a working principle that each ethnic group has or tends to have an individuality of its own and that the members of such a group think, feel, and act primarily as the representatives, so to speak, of that ethnic individuality in which they live, move, and have their being. That is to say, a social as contrasted with individual psychology must, it is held, pronounce both the first and last word regarding all matters of mythology, religion, and art in its numerous forms. The reason is that these are social products, and as such are to be understood only in the light of the laws governing the workings of the collective mind of any particular ethnic group. Such a method is, for instance, employed in Mr. William McDougall's *Social Psychology*, in Mr. R. R. Marett's *Threshold of Religion*,
and in many anthropological articles to be found in *L'Année Sociologique*.

If, therefore, we hold by this new and fruitful method of social psychology we must be prepared to treat the Fairy Faith of the Celtic peoples also in and for itself, as expressive of an individuality more or less unique. It might, indeed, be objected that these people are not a single social group, but rather several such groups, and this is, in a way, true. Nevertheless, their folk-lore displays such remarkable homogeneity, from whatever quarter of the Celtic world it be derived, that it seems the soundest method to treat them as one people for all the purposes of the student of sociology, mythology, and religion.

Granting, then, such a unity in the beliefs of the pan-Celtic race, we are finally obliged to distinguish as it were two aspects thereof. On the one hand, there is shown, even in the mere handful of non-Celtic parallels, which for reasons of space we have been content to cite, as well as in their Celtic equivalents, a generic element common to all peoples living under primitive conditions of society. It is emphatically a social element, but at the same time one which any primitive society is bound to display. On the other hand, in a second aspect, the Celtic beliefs show themselves a character which is wholly Celtic: in the Fairy-Faith, which is generically animistic, we find reflected all sorts of specific characteristics of the Celtic peoples--their patriotism, their peculiar type of imagination, their costumes, amusements, household life, and social and religious customs generally. With this fact in mind, we may proceed to examine certain of the more specialised aspects of the Fairy Faith, as manifested both among Celts and elsewhere.

THE SMALLNESS OF ELVISH SPIRITS AND FAIRIES
Ethnological or Pygmy Theory
In any anthropological estimate of the Fairy Faith, the pygmy stature so commonly attributed to various orders of Celtic and non-Celtic fairies should be considered.

Various scholarly champions of the Pygmy Theory have attempted to explain this smallness of fairies using the hypothesis that the belief in such fairies is due *wholly* to a folk memory of small-statured pre-Celtic races; [1] and

They add that these races, having dwelt in caverns like the prehistoric Caveman, and underground houses like those of Lapps or Eskimos, gave rise to the belief in a fairy world existing in caverns and under hills or mountains. When analysed, our evidence shows that in the majority of cases witnesses have regarded fairies either as non-human nature spirits or else as spirits of the dead; that in a

comparatively limited number of cases they have regarded them as the souls of prehistoric races; and that occasionally they have regarded the belief in them as due to a folk-memory of such races. It follows, then, from such an analysis of evidence, that the Pygmy Theory probably does explain some ethnological elements which have come to be almost inseparably interwoven with the essentially animistic fabric of the primitive fairy faith. But though the theory may so account for such ethnological elements, it disregards the animism that has made such interweaving possible; and, on the whole, we are inclined to accept Mr Jenner's view of the theory since the Pygmy Theory thus fails to provide a basis for what is by far the most important part of the Fairy-Faith, a more adequate theory is required.
Animistic Theory

The testimony of Celtic literature goes to show that leprechauns and similar dwarfish beings are not due to a folk memory of a real pygmy race, that they are spirits like elves, and that the folk memory of a Lappish-like people (who may have been Picts) was confused with them, to result in their being anthropomorphised. Thus, in *Fionn's Ransom*, there is a reference to an undersized Lappish-like man, who may be a Pict; and as Campbell, who records the ancient tale, has observed, there are many similar traditional Highland tales about little men or even about true dwarfs who are good bowmen;

but, certainly, such tales have often blended with other tales, in which supernatural figures like fairies play a role; and the former kind of tales are much more historical and modern in their origin, while the latter are more mythological and extremely archaic. This blending of the natural or ethnological and the supernatural--in quite the same manner as in the modern fairy faith--is seen in another of Campbell's collected tales,

The Lad with the Skin Coverings, which in essence is an other-world tale: a little thickset man in a russet coat,' who is a magician, but who otherwise seems to be a genuine Lapp dressed in furs, is introduced

into a story where real fairy-like beings play the chief parts. Again, in Irish literature, we read of a *loch loch* or 'lake of the pygmies'. Light is thrown upon this reference by what is recorded about the leprechauns and Fergus:--While asleep on the seashore one day, Fergus was about to be carried off by the *luchorpáin*; 'whereat he awoke and caught three of them, to wit, one in each of his two hands, and one on his breast. "Life for life" (i.e. protection), say they. "Let my three wishes (i. e. choices) be given," says Fergus. "Thou shalt have," says the dwarf, "save that which is impossible for us." Fergus requested his knowledge of passing under loughs and links and seas. "Thou shalt have," says the dwarf, "save one which I forbid to thee: thou shalt not go under Lough Rudraide [which] is in thine own country." Thereafter the *lucha rp* (little bodies) put herbs into his ears, and he used to go with them under seas. Others say the dwarf gave his cloak to him, and that Fergus used to put it on his head and thus go under seas. In an etymological comment on this passage, Sir John Rhy^s says:--' The words *chirp* and *luchorpáin* [Anglo-Irish leprechaun] appear to mean literally "small bodies", and the word here rendered
The dwarf is in the Irish *abac,* the etymological equivalent of the Welsh *avanc,* the name by which certain water inhabitants of a mythic nature went in Welsh.
Besides what we find in the recorded Fairy Faith, there are very many parallel traditions, both Celtic and non-Celtic, about various classes of spirits, like leprechauns or other small elvish beings, which Dr. Tylor has called nature spirits; and all of these can best be accounted for using the animistic hypothesis.
For example, in North America (as in Celtic lands) there is no proof of there ever having been an actual dwarf race, but Lewis and Clark, in their *Travels to the Source of the Missouri River*, found among the Sioux a tradition that a hill near the Whitestone River, which the Red Men called the 'Mountain of Little People' or 'Little Spirits', was inhabited by pygmy demons in human form, about eighteen inches

tall, armed with sharp arrows, and ever on the alert to kill mortals who should dare to invade their domain. So afraid were all the tribes of Red Men who lived near the mountain of these little spirits that no one of them could be induced to visit it. And we may compare this American spirit-haunted hill with similar natural hills in Scotland said to be fairy knolls: one near the turning of a road from Reay Wick to Safester, Isle of Unst; one the well-known fairy-haunted Tomnahurich, near Inverness and a third, the hill at Aberfoyle on which the 'people of peace' took the Rev. Robert Kirk when he profaned it by walking on it; or we may equate the American bill with the fairy-haunted Slieve Gullion and Ben Bulbin in Ireland.

The Iroquois had a belief that they could summon dwarfs, who were similar nature spirits, by knocking on a certain large stone. Likewise, the Polong, a Malay familiar spirit, is 'an exceedingly diminutive female figure or mannikin'. East Indian nature spirits, too, are pygmies in stature. In Polynesia, entirely independent of the common legends about wild races of pygmy stature, there are myths about the spirits called *wui* or *vui*, who correspond to European dwarfs and trolls. These little spirits seem to occupy the same position toward the Melanesian gods or culture heroes, Qat of the Banks Islands and Tagaro of the New Hebrides, as daemons toward Greek gods, or as good angels toward the Christian Trinity, or as fairy tribes toward the Brythonic Arthur and the Gaelic hero Cuchulainn. Similarly in Hindu mythology pygmies hold an important place, being sculptured on most temples in company with the gods; e.g. Siva is accompanied by a bodyguard of dwarfs and one of them, the three-legged Bhringi, is a good dancer --like all *corrigans*, pixies, and most fairies.

Beyond the borders of Celtic lands--in Southern Asia with its islands, in Melanesia with New Guinea, and Central African--pygmy races, generally called Negritos, exist in the present day; but they have a fairy faith, just as their normal-sized primitive neighbours have, and it would hardly be reasonable to argue that either of the two fairy-faiths is due to a folk-memory of small-statured peoples. Ancient and thoroughly reliable manuscript records testify to the existence of pygmies in China during the twenty-third century B. C.; yet no one has ever tried to explain the well-known animistic beliefs of modern Chinese men in ghosts, demons, and little nature spirits like fairies, by saying that these are a folk-memory of this ancient pygmy race. In Yezo and the Kuril Islands of Japan still survive a few of the hairy Ainu, a Caucasian-like, under-sized race; and their immediate predecessors; whom they exterminated, were a Negrito race, who, according to some traditions, were two to three feet in stature, and, according to other traditions, only one inch in stature. Both pygmy races, the surviving and the exterminated race, seem independently to have evolved a belief in ghosts and spirits so that here again, it need not be argued that the present pre-Buddhist animism of the Japanese is due to a folk memory of either Sinus or Negritos.

Further examination of the animistic hypothesis designed to explain the smallness of elvish spirits leads away from mere mythology into psychology and sets us on the task of finding out if, after all, primitive ideas about the disembodied human soul may not have originated or at least have helped to shape the Celtic folk conception of fairies as small-statured beings. Mr. A. E. Crawley, in his *Idea of the Soul,* shows by carefully selected evidence from ancient and modern psychologies that 'first among the attributes of the soul in its primary form may be placed its size', and that 'in the majority of cases it is a miniature replica of the person, described often as a mannikin, or homunculus, of a few inches in height'. Sometimes the soul is described as only about three inches in stature. Dr. Frazer shows, likewise, that by practically all contemporary primitive peoples the soul is commonly regarded as a dwarf. The same opinions regarding the human soul prevailed among ancient peoples highly civilised, i.e. the Egyptians and Greeks, and may have thence directly influenced Celtic tradition. Thus, in bas-relief on the Egyptian temple of *Dêr el Bahri*,

Queen Hatshepsû Ra_maka is making offerings of perfume to the gods, while just behind her stands her *Ka* (soul) as a pygmy so little that the crown of its head is just on a level with her waist.
The *Ka* is usually represented as about half the size of an ordinary man.

The Clairvoyance of Mike Farrell.--'Mike Farrell, too, could tell all about the *gentry*, as he lay sick a long time. And he told about Father Brannan's youth, and even the house in Roscommon in which the Father was born; and Father Brannan never said anything more against Mike after that. Mike surely saw the *gentry*; and he was with them during his illness for twelve months. He said they live in *forts* and at Alt Darby ("the Big Rock"). After he got well, he went to America, at the time of the famine.'

The 'Gentry' Army.--' The *gentry* were believed to live up on this hill (Hill of the Brocket Stones, *Clutch-a-brace*), and from it, they would come out like an army and march along the road to the strand. Very few people could see them. They were thought to be like living people but in different dresses. They seemed like soldiers, yet it was known they were not living beings such as we are.'

The Seership of Dan Quinn.--' On Connor's Island (about two miles southward from Cairns by the mainland) my uncle,

Dan Quinn, often used to see big crowds of the *gentry* come into his house and play music and dance. The house would be full of them, but they caused him no fear. Once on such an occasion, one of them came up to him as he lay in bed, and giving him a green leaf told him to put it in his mouth. When he did this, instantly he could not see the *gentry*, but could still hear their music. Uncle Dan always believed he recognized in some of the *gentry* his drowned friends. Only when he was alone would the *gentry* visit him. He was a silent old man, and so never talked much; but I know that this story is as true as can be and that the *gentry* always took an interest in him.'

UNDER THE SHADOW OF BENBULBEN AND BEN WASKIN

I was driving along the BenBulbin road, on the ocean side, with Michael Oates, who was on his way from his mountain-side home to the lowlands to cut hay; and as we looked up at the ancient mountain, so mysterious and silent in the shadows and fog of a calm early morning of summer, he told me about its invisible inhabitants:--

The 'Gentry' Huntsmen.--'I knew a man who saw the *gentry* hunting on the other side of the mountain. He saw hounds and horsemen cross the road and jump the hedge in front of him, and it was one o'clock at night. The next day he passed the place again, and looked for the tracks of the huntsmen, but saw not a trace of tracks at all.'

The 'Taking' of the Turf-Cutter.--After I had heard about two boys who were drowned opposite Inishmurray, and who afterwards appeared as apparitions, for the *gentry* had them, this curious story was related:--'A man was cutting turf out on the side of Benbulben when a strange man came to him and said, "You have cut enough turf for to-day. You had better stop and go home." The turf-cutter looked around in surprise, and in two seconds the strange man had disappeared, but he decided to go home. And as soon as he was home, such a feeling came over him that he could not tell whether he was alive or dead. Then he took to his bed and never rose again. *Hearing the 'Gentry' Music.*--At this Michael said to his companion in the cart with us, William Barber, 'You tell how you heard the music'; and this followed:--'One night, about one o'clock, myself and another young man were passing along the road up there round Ben Bulbin when we heard the finest kind of music. All sorts of music seemed to be playing. We could see nothing at all, though we thought we heard voices like children's. It was the music of the *gentry* we heard.'

My next friend to testify is Pat Ruddy, eighty years old, one of the most intelligent and prosperous farmers living beside Ben Bulben. He greeted me in the true Irish way, but before we could come to talk about fairies his good wife induced me to enter another room where she had secretly prepared a great feast spread out on a fresh white cloth, while Pat and myself had been exchanging ols about America and Ireland. When I returned to the kitchen the whole family were assembled round the blazing turf fire, and Pat was soon talking about the 'gentry':--

Seeing the 'Gentry' Army.--'Old people used to say the *gentry* were in the mountains; that is certain, but I never could be quite sure of it myself. One night, however, near midnight, I did have a sight: I set out from Bantrillick to come home, and near Ben Bulben there was the greatest army you ever saw, five or six thousand of them in armour shining in the moonlight. A strange man rose out of the hedge and stopped me, for a minute, in the middle of the road. He looked into my face, and then let me go.'

An Ossianic Fragment.--' A man went away with the *good people* (or *gentry*) and returned to find the townland all in ruins. As he came back riding on a horse of the *good people*, he saw some men in a quarry trying to move a big stone. He helped them with it, but his saddle girth broke, and he fell to the ground. The horse ran away, and he was left there, by an old man.

SCHOOLMASTER'S TESTIMONY

A schoolmaster, who is a native of the BenBulbin country, offers this testimony:--' There is an implicit belief here in the *gentry*, especially among the old people. They consider them the spirits of their departed relations and friends, who visit them in joy and sorrow. On the death of a member of a family, they believe the spirits of their near relatives are present; they do not see them but feel their presence. They even have a strong belief that the spirits show them the future in dreams; and say that cases of affl, are always foreshown in a dream.

'The belief in changelings is not now generally prevalent; but in olden times a mother used to place a pair of iron tongs over the cradle before leaving the child alone, in order that the fairies should not change the child for a weak one of their own. It was another custom to take a wisp of straw, and, lighting one end of it, make a fiery sign of the cross over a cradle before a babe could be placed in it.'

WITH THE IRISH MYSTICS IN THE *SIDHE* WORLD

Let us now turn to the Rosses Point country, which, as we have already said, is one of the very famous places for seeing the' gentry', or, as educated Irish seers who make pilgrimages thither call them, the *Slake*. I have been told by more than one such seer that there on the hills and Greenlands (a great stretch of open country, treeless and grass-grown), and on the strand at Lower Rosses Point--called Wren Point by the country-folk--these beings country found their wonderful music heard; and a well-known Irish artist has shown me many drawings, and paintings in oil, of these *Sidhe* people as he has often beheld them at those

places and elsewhere in Ireland. They are described as a race of majestic appearance and marvellous beauty, in form human, yet in nature divine. The highest order of them seems to be a race of beings evolved to a superhuman plane of existence, such as the ancients called gods; and with this opinion, strange as it may seem in this age, all the educated Irish seers with whom I have been privileged to talk agree, though they go further, and say that these highest *Sidhe* races still inhabiting Ireland are the ever-young, immortal divine race known to the ancient men of Erin as the Tuatha De Danann.

Of all European lands I venture to say that Ireland is the most mystical, and, in the eyes of true Irishmen, as much the Magic Island of Gods and Initiates now as it was when the Sacred Fires flashed from its purple, heather-covered mountain-tops and mysterious round towers, and the Greater Mysteries drew to its hallowed shrines neophytes from the West as well as from the East, from India and Egypt as well as from Atlantis; [1] and Erin's mystic-seeing sons still watch and wait for the relighting of the Fires and the restoration of the old Druidic Mysteries. Herein I but imperfectly echo the mystic message Ireland's seers gave me, a pilgrim to their Sacred Isle. And until this mystic message is interpreted, men cannot discover the secret of Gaelic myth and song in olden or in modern times, they cannot drink at the ever-flowing fountain of Gaelic genius, the perennial source of inspiration which lies behind the new revival of literature and art in Ireland, nor understand the seeming reality of the fairy races.

AN IRISH MYSTIC'S TESTIMONY

Through the kindness of an Irish mystic, who is a seer, I am enabled to present here, in the form of a dialogue, very rare and very important evidence, which will serve to illustrate and to confirm what has just been paid above about the mysticism of Ireland. To anthropologists, this evidence may be of more than ordinary value when they know that

it comes from one who is not only a cultured seer but who is also a man conspicuously successful in the practical life of a great city:--

Visions.--

Q.--Are all visions which you have had of the same character?

A.--'I have always made a distinction between pictures seen in the memory of nature and visions of actual beings now existing in the inner world. We can make the same distinction in our world: I may close my eyes and see you as a vivid picture in memory, or I may look at you with my physical eyes and see your actual image. In seeing these beings of which I speak, the physical eyes may be open or closed: mystical beings in their own world and nature are never seen with the physical eyes.'

Otherworlds.--

Q.--By the inner world do you mean the Celtic Otherworld?

A.--'Yes; though there are many Other Worlds. The *Tir-na-nog* of the ancient Irish, in which the races of the *Sidhe* exist, may be described as a radiant archetype of this world, though this definition does not at all express its psychic nature. In *Tir-na-nog* one sees nothing save harmony and beautiful forms. There are other worlds in which we can see horrible shapes.'

Classification of the 'Sidhe'.--

Q.--Do you in any way classify the *Sidhe* races to which you refer?

A.--'The beings whom I call the *Sidhe*, I divide, as I have seen them, into two great classes: those which are shining, and those which are opalescent and seem lit up by a light within themselves. The shining beings appear to be lower in the hierarchies; the opalescent beings are more rarely seen, and appear to hold the positions of great chiefs or princes among the tribes of Dana.'

Conditions of Seership.--

Q.--Under what state or condition and where have you seen such beings?

A.--'I have seen them most frequently after being away from a city or town for a few days. The whole west coast of Ireland from Donegal to

Kerry seems charged with a magical power, and I find it easiest to see while I am there. I have always found it comparatively easy to see visions while at ancient monuments like NewGrange and Dowth, because I think such places are naturally charged with psychical forces, and were for that reason made use of long ago as sacred places. I usually find it possible to throw myself into the mood of seeing; but sometimes visions have forced themselves upon me.'

The Shining Beings.--

Q.--Can you describe the shining beings?

A.--'It is very difficult to give any intelligible description of them. The first time I saw them with great vividness I was lying on a hill-side alone in the west of Ireland, in County Sligo: I had been listening to music in the air, and to what seemed to be the sound of bells, and was trying to understand these aerial clashings in which wind seemed to break upon wind in an ever-changing musical silvery sound. Then the space before me grew luminous, and I began to see one beautiful being after another.'

The Opalescent Beings.--

Q.--Can you describe one of the opalescent beings?

A.--' The first of these I saw I remember very clearly, and the manner of its appearance: there was at first a dazzle of light, and then I saw that this came from the heart of a tall figure with a body shaped out of half-transparent or opalescent air, and throughout the body ran a radiant, electrical fire, to which the heart seemed the centre. Around the head of this being and through its waving luminous hair, which was blown all about the body like living strands of gold, there appeared flaming wing-like auras. From the being itself, light seemed to stream outwards in every direction; and the effect left on me after the vision was one of extraordinary lightness, joyousness, or ecstasy.

'At about this same period of my life, I saw many of these

great beings and I then thought that I had visions of Aengus, Manannan, Lug, and other famous kings or princes among the Tuatha De Danann; but since then I have seen so many beings of a similar character that I now no longer would attribute to any one of them personal identity with particular beings of legend; though I believe that they correspond in a general way to the Tuatha De Danann or ancient Irish gods.'

The stature of the 'Sidhe'.--

Q.--You speak of the opalescent beings as great beings; what stature do you assign to them, and the shining beings?

A.--'The opalescent beings seem to be about fourteen feet in stature, though I do not know why I attribute to them such definite height, since I had nothing to compare them with; but I have always considered them as much taller than our race. The shining beings seem to be about our own stature or just a little taller. Peasant and other Irish seers do not usually speak of the *Sidhe* as being little, but as being tall: an old schoolmaster in the West of Ireland described them to me from his own visions as tall beautiful people, and he used some Gaelic words, which I took as meaning that they were shining with every colour.'

The worlds of the 'Sidhe.'--

Q.--Do the two orders of *Sidhe* beings inhabit the same world?

A.--'The shining beings belong to the mid-world; while the opalescent beings belong to the heaven-world. There are three great worlds which we can see while we are still in the body: the earth-world, mid-world, and heaven-world.'

Nature of the 'Sidhe.'--

Q.--Do you consider the life and state of these *Sidhe* beings superior to the life and state of men?

A.--' I could never decide. One can say that they are certainly more beautiful than men are, and that their worlds seem more beautiful than our world.

'Among the shining orders there does not seem to be any individualised life: thus if one of them raises his hands all raise their hands, and if one drinks from a fire-fountain all do; they seem to move and to have their real existence in a being higher than themselves, to which they are a kind of body. Theirs is, I think, a collective life, so individualised and so calm that I might have more varied thoughts in five hours than they would have in five years; and yet one feels an extraordinary purity and, exaltation about their life. Beauty of form with them has never been broken up by the passions which arise in the developed egotism of human beings. A hive of bees has been described as a single organism with disconnected cells; and some of these tribes of shining beings seem to be little more than one being manifesting itself in many beautiful forms. I speak this with reference to the shining beings only: I think that among the opalescent or *Sidhe* beings, in the heaven-world, there is an even closer spiritual unity, but also a greater individuality.'

Influence of the 'Sidhe' on Men.--

Q.--Do you consider any of these *Sidhe* beings inimical to humanity?

A.--'Certain kinds of the shining beings, whom I call wood beings, have never affected me with any evil influences I could recognize. But the water beings, also of the shining tribes, I always dread, because I felt whenever I came into contact with them a great drowsiness of mind and, I often thought, an actual drawing away of vitality.'

Water Beings Described.--

Q.--Can you describe one of these water beings?

A.--'In the world under the waters--under a lake in the West of Ireland in this case--I saw a blue and orange coloured king seated on a throne; and there seemed to be some fountain of mystical fire rising from under his throne, and he breathed this fire into himself as though it were his life. As I looked, I saw groups of pale beings, almost grey in colour, coming down one side of the throne by the fire-fountain. They placed their head and lips near the heart of the elemental king, and, then, as they touched him, they shot upwards, plumed and radiant, and passed on the other side, as though they had received a new life from this chief of their world.'

Wood Beings Described.--

Q.--Can you describe one of the wood beings?

A.--'The wood beings I have seen most often are of a shining silvery colour with a tinge of blue or pale violet, and with dark purple-coloured hair.'

Reproduction and Immortality of the 'Sidhe'.--

Q.--Do you consider the races of the *Sidhe* able to reproduce their kind; and are they immortal?

A.--' The higher kinds seem capable of breathing forth beings out of themselves, but I do not understand how they do so. I have seen some of them who contain elemental beings within themselves, and these they could send out and receive back within themselves again.

'The immortality ascribed to them by the ancient Irish is only a relative immortality, their space of life being much greater than ours. In time, however, I believe that they grow old and then pass into new bodies just as men do, but whether by birth or by the growth of a new body I cannot say, since I have no certain knowledge about this.'

Sex among the 'Sidhe'—

Q.—Does sexual differentiation seem to prevail among the Sidhe races?

A.—'I have seen forms both male and female, and forms which did not suggest sex at all.'

'Sidhe' and Human Life.—

Q.—(1) is it possible, as the ancient Irish thought, that certain of the higher *Sidhe* beings have entered or could enter our plane of life by submitting to human birth?) On the other hand, do you consider it possible for men in trance or at death to enter the *Sidhe* world?

A.—(1) 'I cannot say.' 'Yes; both in trance and after death. I think any one who thought much of the *Sidhe* during his life and who saw them frequently and brooded on them would likely go to their world after death.'

Social Organization of the 'Sidhe'.—

Q.—You refer to chieftain-like or prince-like beings, and a king among water beings; is there therefore definite social organisation among the various *Sidhe* orders and races, and if so, what is its nature?

A.—'I cannot say about a definite social organisation. I have seen beings who seemed to command others, and who were held in reverence. This implies an organisation, but whether it is instinctive like that of a hive of bees, or consciously organised like human society, I cannot say.'

Lower 'Sidhe' as Nature Elementals.--

Q.--You speak of the water-being king as an elemental king; do you suggest thereby a resemblance between lower *Sidhe* orders and what mediaeval mystics called elementals?

A.--'The lower orders of the *Sidhe* are, I think, the natural elementals of the mediaeval mystics.'

Nourishment of the Higher 'Sidhe'.--

Q.--The water beings as you have described them seem to be nourished and kept alive by something akin to electrical fluids; do the higher orders of the *Sidhe* seem to be similarly nourished?

A.--'They seemed to me to draw their life out of the Soul of the World.'

Collective Visions of 'Sidhe' Beings.--

Q.--Have you had visions of the various *Sidhe* beings in company with other persons?

A.--'I have had such visions on several occasions.'

This statement has been confirmed to me by three participants in such collective visions, who separately at different times have seen in company with our witness the same vision at the same moment. On another occasion, on the Greenlands at Rosses Point, County Sligo, the same

Sidhe being was seen by our present witness and a friend with him, also possessing the faculty of seership, at a time when the two recipients were some little distance apart, and they hurried to each other to describe the being, not knowing that the explanation was mutually unnecessary. I have talked with both recipients so much, and know them so intimately that I am fully able to state that as recipients they fulfil all necessary pathological conditions required by psychologists to make their evidence acceptable.

PARALLEL EVIDENCE AS TO THE *SIDHE* RACES

In general, the rare evidence above recorded from the Irish seer could be paralleled by similar evidence from at least two other reliable Irish people, with whom also I have been privileged to discuss the Fairy Faith. One is a member of the Faithful Irish Academy, the other is the wife of a well-known Irish historian, and both of them testify to having likewise had collective visions of *Sidhe* beings in Ireland.

This is what Mr. William B. Yeats wrote to me, while this study was in progress, concerning the Celtic Fairy Kingdom:--'I am certain that it exists, and will someday be studied as it was studied by Kirk.'[1]

INDEPENDENT EVIDENCE FROM THE *SIDHE* WORLD

One of the most remarkable discoveries of our Celtic research has been that the native population of the Rosses Point country, or, as we have called it, the *Sidhe* world, in most essentials, and, what is most important, by independent folk testimony, substantiate folk testimony and statements of the educated Irish mystics to whom we have just referred, as follows:--

John Conway's Vision of the 'Gentry'.--In Upper Rosses Point, Mrs. J. Conway told me this about the 'gentry':--'John Conway, my husband, who was a pilot by profession,

in watching for in-coming ships used to go up on the high hill among the Fairy Hills; and there he often saw the *gentry* going down the hill to the strand. One night in particular he recognized them as men and women of the *gentry* and they were as big as any living people. It was late at night about forty years ago.'

Ghosts and Fairies.--When first I introduced myself to Owen Conway, in his bachelor quarters, a cosy cottage at Upper Rosses Point, he said that Mr. W. B. Yeats and other men famous in Irish literature had visited him to hear about the fairies, and though he knew very little about the fairies he nevertheless always liked to talk of them. Then Owen began to tell me about a man's ghost which both he and Bran Reggan had seen at different times on the road to Sligo, then about a woman's ghost which he and other people had often seen near where we were, and then about the exercising of a haunted house in Sligo some sixty years ago by Father McGowan, who as a result died soon afterwards, apparently having been killed by the exorcised spirits. Finally, I heard from him the following anecdotes about the fairies:--

A Stone Wall overthrew by 'Fairy' Agency.--'Nothing is more certain than that there are fairies. The old folks always thought them the fallen angels. At the back of this house, the fairies had their pass. My neighbour started to build a cow-shed, and one wall abutting on the pass was thrown down twice, and nothing but the fairies ever did it. The third time the wall was built it stood.'

Fairies passing through Stone Walls.--'Where MacEwen's house stands was a noted fairy place. Men in the building saw fairies on horses coming across the spot, and the stone walls did not stop them at all.'

Seeing the 'Gentry'.--' A cousin of mine, who was a pilot, once went to the watch-house up there on the Point to take his brother's place; and he saw ladies coming towards him as he crossed the Greenlands. At first, he thought they were coming from a dance, but there was no dance going on then, and, if there had been, no human beings dressed like them and moving as they were could have come from any part of the globe, and in so great a party, at that hour of the night. Then when they passed him and he saw how beautiful they were, he knew them for the *gentry* women.'

'Michael Reddy (our next witness) saw the *gentry* down on the Greenlands in regimentals like an army, and in daylight. He was a young man at the time, and had been sent out to see if any cattle were astray.'

And this is what Michael Reddy, of Rosses Point, now a sailor on the ship *Tartar*, sailing from Sligo to neighbouring ports on the Irish coast, asserts in confirmation of Owen Conway's statement about him:--'I saw the *gentry* on the strand (at Lower Rosses Point) about forty years ago. It was afternoon. I first saw one of them like an officer pointing at me what seemed like a sword; and when I got on the Greenlands I saw a great company of *gentry*, like soldiers, in red, laughing and shouting. Their leader was a big man, and they were ordinary human size. As a result [of this vision] I took to my bed and lay there for weeks. On another occasion, late at night, I was with my mother milking cows, and we heard the *gentry* all around us talking, but could not see them.'

Going to the 'Gentry' through Death, Dreams, or Trance.--John Conway, one of the most reliable citizens of Upper Rosses Point, offers the following testimony concerning the 'gentry':--'In olden times the *gentry* were very numerous about *forts* and here on the Greenlands, but rarely seen. They appeared to be the same as any living man. When people died it was said the *gentry* took them, for they would afterwards appear among the *gentry*.'

"We had a ploughman of good habits who came in one day too late for his morning's work, and he very seriously said, "May be if you had travelled all night as much as I have you wouldn't talk. I was away with the *gentry*, and save for a lady I couldn't have been back now. I saw a long hall full of many people. Some of them I knew and some I did not know. The lady saved me by telling me to eat no food there, however enticing it might be."'

'A young man at Drumcliffe was *taken* [in a trance state], and was with the *Daoine Maithe* some time, and then got back. Another man, whom I knew well, was haunted by the *gentry* for a long time, and he often went off with *them* (apparently in a dream-themrance state).

'Sidhe' Music.--The story which now follows substantiates the testimony of cultured Irish seers that at Lower Rosses Point the music of the *Sidhe* can be heard:--'Three women were gathering shell-fish, in the month of March, on the lowest point of the strand (Lower Rosses or Wren Point) when they heard the most beautiful music. They set to work to dance with it, and danced themselves sick. They then thanked the invisible musician and went home.'

THE TESTIMONY OF A COLLEGE PROFESSOR

Our next witness is the Rev. Father--'a professor in a Catholic college in West Ireland, most of his statements are based on events which happened among his acquaintances and relatives, and his deductions are the result of careful investigation:--

Apparitions from Fairyland.--'Some twenty to thirty years ago, on the borders of County Roscommon near County Sligo, according to the firm belief of one of my relatives, a sister of his was *taken* by the fairies on her desi wedding night; she appea wedding night there afterwards as an apparition. She seemed to want to speak, but her mother, who was in bed at the time, was thoroughly frightened and turned her face to the wall. The mother is convinced that she saw this apparition of her daughter, and my relative thinks she might have saved her.

'This same relative who gives it as his opinion that his sister was *taken* by the fairies, at a different time saw the apparition of another relative of mine who also, according to similar belief, had been *taken* by the fairies when only five years old. The child-apparition appeared beside its living sister one day while the sister was going from the yard into the house, and it followed her in. It is said the child was *taken* because she was such a good girl.'

Nature of the Belief in Fairies.--' As children, we were always afraid of fairies and were taught to say "God bless *them*! God bless *them*!" whenever we heard them mentioned.

'In our family, we always made it a point to have clean water in the house at night for the fairies.

'If anything like dirty water was thrown out of doors after dark it was necessary to say "*Hugga, hugga salach*!" as a warning to the fairies not to get their clothes wet.

'Untasted food, like milk, used to be left on the table at night for the fairies. If you were eating and food fell from you, it was not right to take it back, for the fairies wanted it. Many families are very serious about this even now. The luckiest thing to do in such cases is to pick up the food and eat just a speck of it and then throw the rest away to the fairies.

'Ghosts and apparitions are commonly said to live in isolated thorn-bushes, or thorn-trees. Many lonely bushes of this kind have their ghosts. For example, there is Fanny's Bush, Sally's Bush, and another I know of in County Sligo near Boyle.'

Personal Opinions.--'The fairies of any one race are the people of the preceding race--the Fomors for the Fir Bolgs, the Fir Bolgs for the Dananns, and the Dananns for us. The old races died. Where did they go? They became spirits--and fairies. Second-sight gave our race power to see the inner world. When Christianity came to Ireland the people had no *definite* heaven. Before, their ideas about the other world were vague. But the older ideas of a spirit world remained side by side with the Christian ones, and being preserved in a subconscious way gave rise to the fairy world.'

EVIDENCE FROM COUNTY ROSCOMMON

Our next place for investigation will be the ancient province of the great fairy fairy queen, who made fairy queenous by leading against Cuchulainn the united armies of four of the five provinces of Ireland, and all on account of a bull which she coveted. And there could be no better part of it to visit than Roscommon, which Dr Douglas Hyde has made popular in Irish folk-lore.

Dr. Hyde and the Leprechaun.--One day while I was privileged to be at Ratra, Dr. Hyde invited me to walk with him in the country. After we had visited an old *fort* which belonged to the 'good people', and had noticed some other of their haunts in that part of Queen Maeve's realm, we entered a straw-thatched cottage on the roadside and found the good house-wife and her fine-looking daughter both at home. In response to Dr. Hyde's inquiries, the mother stated that one day, in her girlhood, near a hedge from which she was gathering wild berries, she saw a leprechaun in a hole under a stone:--' He wasn't much larger than a doll, and he was most perfectly formed, with a little mouth and eyes.' Nothing was told about the little fellow having a myonemoney bag though the woman money people told her afterwards that she would have been rich if she had only had sense enough to catch him when she had a good chance.

The Death Coach.

The next tale the mother told was about the death coach who used to pass by the very house we were in. Every night until after her daughter was born she used to rise on her elbow in bed to listen to the death coach passing by. It passed about midnight, and she could hear the rushing, the tramping of the horses, and the most beautiful singing, just like fairy music, but she could not understand the words. Once or twice she was brave enough to open the door and look out as the coach passed, but she could never see a thing, though there was

the noise and singing. One time a man had to wait on the roadside to let the fairy horses go by, and he could hear their passing very clearly, and couldn't see one of them.

When we got home, Dr. Hyde told me that the fairies of the region are rarely seen. The people usually say that they hear or feel them only.

The 'Good People' and Mr. Gilleran.--After the mother had testified, the daughter, who is quite of the younger generation, gave her own opinion. She said that the 'good people' live in the *forts* and often take men and women or youths who pass by the *forts* after sunset; that Mr Gilleran, who died not long ago, once saw certain dead friends and recognized among them those who were believed to have been *taken* and those who died naturally, and that he saw them again when he was on his death-bed.

We have here, as in so many other accounts, a clear connection between the realm of the dead and Fairyland.

THE TESTIMONY OF A LOUGH DERG SEER

Neil Colton, seventy-three years old, who lives in Tamlach Townland, on the shores of Lough Derg, County Donegal, has a local reputation for having seen the 'gentle folk', and so I called upon him. As we sat around his blazing turf fire, and amid his family of three sturdy boys--for he married late in life--this is what he related:--

A Girl Recovered from Faerie.--'One day, just before sunset in midsummer, and I was a boy then, my brother and cousin and myself were gathering bilberries (whortleberries) up by the rocks at the back of here, when all at once we heard music. We hurried round the rocks, and there we were within a few hundred feet of six or eight of the *gentle folk*, and they were dancing. When they saw us, a little woman dressed all in red came running out from them towards us, and she struck my cousin across the face with what seemed to be a green rush. We ran for home as hard as we could, and when my cousin reached the house she fell dead. Father saddled a horse and went for Father Ryan. When Father Ryan arrived, he put a stole about his neck and began praying

over my cousin and reading psalms and striking her with the stole; and in that way brought her back. He said if she had not caught hold of my brother, she would have been *taken* for ever.'

The 'Gentle Folk'.--'The *gentle folk* are not earthly people; they are a people with a nature of their own. Even in the water there are men and women of the same character. Others have caves in the rocks, and in them rooms and apartments. These races were terribly plentiful a hundred years ago, and they'll come back again. My father lived two miles from here, where there were plenty of the *gentle folk*. In olden times they used to take young folks and keep them and draw all the life out of their bodies. Nobody could ever tell their nature exactly.'

EVIDENCE FROM COUNTY FERMANAGH

From James Summerville, eighty-eight years old, who lives in the country near Irvinestown, I heard much about the 'wee people' and banshees, and then the following remarkable story concerning the 'good people':--

Travelling Clairvoyance through 'Fairy' Agency.--' From near Ederney, County Fermanagh, about seventy years ago, a man whom I knew well was taken to America on Hallow Eve Night; and *they* (the *good people*) made him look down a chimney to see his daughter cooking at a kitchen fire. Then *they* took him to another place in America, where he saw a friend he knew. The next morning he was at his own home here in Ireland.

'This man wrote a letter to his daughter to know if she was at the place and at work on Halloween Eve Night, and she wrote back that she was. He was sure that it was the *good people* who had taken him to America and back in one night.'

EVIDENCE FROM COUNTY ANTRIM

At the request of Major R. G. Berry, M.R.I.A., of Richhill Castle, Armagh, Mr H. Higginson, of Glenavy, County Antrim, collected all the material he could find concerning the fairy traditions part fairy tradition, and sent

to me the results, from which I have selected the very interesting, and, in some respects, unique tales which follow:--

The Fairies and the Weaver.--'Ned Judge, of Sophy's Bridge, was a weaver. Every night after he went to bed the weaving started by itself, and when he arose in the morning he would find the dressing which had been made ready for weaving so broken and entangled that it took him hours to put it right. Yet with all this drawback he got no poorer, because the fairies left him plenty of household necessaries, and whenever he sold a web [of cloth] he always received treble the amount bargained for.'

Meeting Two Regiments of 'Them'.--'William Megarry, of Ballinderry, as his daughter who is married to James Megarry, J.P., told me, was one night going to Crumlin on horseback for a doctor, when after passing through Glenavy he met just opposite the Vicarage two regiments of *them* (the fairies) coming along the road towards Glenavy. One regiment was dressed in red and one in blue or green uniform. *They* were playing music, but when they opened out to let him pass through the middle of *them* the music ceased until he had passed by.'

IN CUCHULAINN'S COUNTRY: A CIVIL ENGINEER'S TESTIMONY

In the heroic days of pagan Ireland, as tradition tells, the ancient earthworks, now called the Navan Rings, just outside Armagh, were the stronghold of Cuchulainn and the Red Branch Knights; and, later, under Patrick, Armagh itself, one of the old mystic centres of Erin, became the ecclesiastical capital of the Gaels. And from this romantic country, one of its best-informed native sons, a graduate civil engineer of Dublin University, offers the following important evidence:--

The Fairies are the Dead.--' When I was a youngster near Armagh, I was kept good by being told that the fairies could take bad boys away. The sane belief about the fairies, however, is different, as I discovered when I grew up. The old people in County Armagh seriously believe that the

fairies are the spirits of the dead, and they say that if you have many friends deceased you have many friendly fairies, or if you have many enemies deceased you have many fairies looking out to do you harm.'

Food-Offerings to Place-Fairies.--'It was very usual formerly, and the practice is not yet given up, to place a bed, some other furniture, and plenty of food in a newly-constructed dwelling the night before the time fixed for moving into it; and if the food is not consumed, and the crumbs swept up by the door in the morning, the house cannot safely be occupied. I know of two houses now that have never been occupied, because the fairies did not show their willingness and goodwill by taking food offered to them.'

ON THE SLOPES OF SLIEVE GULLION

In climbing to the summit of Cuchulainn's mountain, which overlooks parts of the territory made famous by the 'Cattle Raid of Cooley', I met John O'Hare, sixty-eight years old, of Longfield Townland, leading his horse to pasture, and I stopped to talk with him about the 'good people'.

'The *good people* in this mountain,' he said, 'are the people who have died and been *taken*; the mountain is enchanted.'

The 'Fairy' Overflowing of the Meal-Chest.--'An old woman came to the wife of Steven Callaghan and told her not to let Steven cut a certain hedge. "It is where we shelter at night," the old woman added; and Mrs. Callaghan recognized the old woman as one who had been *taken* in confinement. A few nights later the same old woman appeared to Mrs. Callaghan and asked for charity; and she was offered some meal, which she did not take. Then she asked for lodgings, but did not stop. When Mrs. Callaghan saw the meal-chest next morning it was overflowing with meal: it was the old woman's gift for the hedge.'

THE TESTIMONY OF TWO DOMINATE PERCIPIENTS

After my friend, the Rev. Father L. Donnellan, C.C., of Dromintee, County Armagh, had introduced me to Alice Cunningham, of his parish, and she had told much about the 'gentle folk', she emphatically declared that they do exist--and this in the presence of Father Donnellan--because she has often seen them on Carrickbroad Mountain, near where she lives. And she then reported as follows concerning enchanted Slieve Gullion:--

The 'Sidhe' Guardian of Slieve Gullion.--'The top of Slieve Gullion is a very *gentle* place. A fairy has her house there by the lake, but she is invisible. She interferes with nobody. I hear of no *gentler* places here than Carrickbroad and Slieve Gullion.'

Father Donnellan and I called next upon Thomas McCrink and his wife at Carrifamayan because Mrs. McCrink claims to have seen some of the good people, and this their people--

Nature of the 'Good People'.--'I've heard and felt the *good people* coming on the wind, and I once saw them down in the middle field on my father's place playing football. They are still on earth. Among them are the spirits of our ancestors; and these rejoice whenever good fortune comes our way, for I saw them before my mother won her land [after a long legal contest] in the field rejoicing.

'Some of the *good people* I have thought of were fallen angels, though these may be dead people whose time is not up. We are only like shadows in this world: my mother died in England, and she came to me in the spirit. I saw her plainly. I ran to catch her, but my hands ran through her form as if it were mere mist. Then there was a crack, and she was gone.' And, finally, after a moment, our recipient said:--'The fairies once passed down this lane here on a Christmas morning; and I took them to be suffering souls out of Purgatory, going to mass.'

THE TESTIMONY OF A DOMINATE SEERESS

Father Donnellan, the following day, took me to talk with almost the oldest woman in his parish, Mrs. Biddy Grant, eighty-six years old, of Upper Youghal, beside Slieve Gullion. Mrs. Grant is a fine specimen of an Irishwoman, with white hair, a clear complexion, and an expression of great natural intelligence, though now somewhat feeble from age. Her

mind is yet clear, however; and her testimony is substantiated by this statement from her daughter, who lives with her:--'My mother has the power of seeing things. It is a fact with her that spirits exist. She has seen much, even in her old age; and what she is always telling me scares me half to death.'

The following is Mrs. Grant's direct testimony given at her own home, on September 20, 1909, in answer to our question if she knew anything about the 'good people'

Seeing the 'Good People' as the Dead.--' I saw *them* once as plain as can be--big, little, old, and young. I was in bed at the time, and a boy whom I had raised since he was born was lying ill beside me. Two of *them* came and looked at him; then came in three of *them*. One of *them* seemed to have something like a book, and he put his hand to the boy's mouth; then he went away, while others appeared, opening the back window to make an avenue through the house; and through this avenue came great crowds. At this, I shook the boy, and said to him, "Do you see anything?" "No," he said; but as I made him look a second time he said, "I do." After that, he got well.

'These *good people* were the spirits of our dead friends, but I could not recognize them. I have often seen them that way while in my bed. Many women are among them. I once touched a boy of theirs, and he was just like feathers in my hand; there was no substance in him, and I knew he wasn't a living being. I don't know where they live; I've heard they live in the *Carriage* (rocks). Many times I've heard of them *taking* people or leading them astray. They can't live far away when they come to me in such a rush. They are as big as we are. I think these fairy people are all through this country and in the mountains.'

An Apparition of a' Sidhe' Woman?--' At a wake, I went out of doors at midnight and saw a woman running up and down the field with a strange light in her hand. I called out to my daughter, but she saw nothing, though all the time the woman dressed in white was in the field, shaking the light and running back and forth as fast as you could wink.

I thought the woman might be the spirit of Nancy Frink, but I was not sure.'

(EVIDENCE FROM LOUGH GUR, COUNTY LIMERICK)

One of the most interesting parts of Ireland for the archaeologist and the folklorist alike is the territory immediately surrounding Lough Gur, County Limerick. Shut in for the most part from the outer world by a circle of low-lying hills on whose summits fairy goddesses yet dwell invisibly, this region, famous for its numerous and well-preserved cromlechs, dolmens, menhirs, and tumuli, and for the rare folk-traditions current among its peasantry, has long been popularly regarded as a sort of Otherworld preserve haunted by fairy beings, who dwell both in its waters and on its land.

There seems to be no reasonable doubt that in pre-Christian times the Lough Gur country was a very sacred spot, a mystic centre for pilgrimages and the celebration of Celtic religious rites, including those of initiation. The Lough is still enchanted, but once in seven years the spell passes off it, and it then appears like dry land to anyone fortunate anyone beholds it. At such a time of disenchantment, a Tree is seen growing up through the lake bottom--a Tree like the strange world tree of Scandinavian myth. The Tree is covered with a Green Cloth, and under it sits the lake's guardian, a woman knitting. [1] The peasantry about Lough Gur still believes that beneath its waters there is one of the chief entrances in Ireland to *Tir-na-nog*, the 'Land of Youth', the Fairy Realm. And when a child is stolen by the Munster fairies, 'Lough Gur is conjectured to be the place of its unearthly transmutation from the human to the fairy state.'[1]

To my friend, Count John de Salis, of Balliol College, I am indebted for the following legendary material, collected by him on the fairy-haunted Lough Gur estate, his ancestral home, and annotated by the Rev. J. F. Lynch, one of the best-informed antiquarians living in that part of South Ireland

The Fairy Goddesses, Aine--and Fennel (or Finnen).--' There are two hills near Lough Gur upon whose summit sacrifices and sacred rites used to be celebrated according to living tradition. One, about three miles southwest of the lake, is southwest Aine, Aine or Ane being the name of an ancient Irish goddess, derived from *a* "bright." The other, the highest hill on the lake-shores, is called Knock Luke shoresHill of the Goddess Fennel, from *Finnen* or *Finnine* or *Fininne*, a form of *fin*, "white." The peasantry of the region calls Aine one of the Good People;[1] and they say that

Fennel (her sister goddess or a variant of herself) lived on the top of Knock Fennel' (termed Finnen in a State Paper dated 1200).

The Fairy Boat-Race.--'Different old peasants have told me that on clear calm moonlight nights in summer, fairy boats appear racing across Lough Gur. The boats come from the eastern side of the lake, and when they have arrived at Garrod Island, where the Desmond Castle lies in ruins, they vanish behind Knock Adoon. There are four of these phantom boats, and in each, there are two men rowing and a woman steering. No sound is heard, though the seer can see the weird silvery splash of the oars and the churning of the water at the bows of the boats as they shoot along. It is evident that they are racing, because one boat gets ahead of the others, and all the rowers can be seen straining at the oars. Boats and occupants seem to be transparent, and you

cannot see exactly what their nature is. One old peasant told me that it is the shining brightness of the clothes on the phantom rowers and on the women who steer which makes them visible.

'Another man, who is about forty years of age, and as far as I know of good habits, assures me that he also has seen this fairy boat-race, and that it can still be seen at the proper season.'

The Bean-Tighe. [1]--' The *Bean-tighe*, the fairy housekeeper of the enchanted submerged castle of the Earl of Desmond, is supposed to appear sitting on art ancient earthen monument shaped like a great chair and hence called *Suidheachan,* the "Housekeeper's Little Seat," on Knock Adoon (Hill of the Fort), which juts out into the Lough. The *Bean-Tighe,* as I have heard an old peasant tell the tale, was once asleep on her Seat, when the *Buachaille* [2] or "Little Herd Boy"

stole her golden comb. When the *Bean-Tighe* awoke and saw what had happened, she cast a curse upon the cattle of the *Buachailleen,* and soon all of them were dead, and then the "Little Herd Boy" himself died, but before his death, he ordered the golden comb to be cast into the Lough.'

Lough Gur Fairies in General.--' The peasantry in the Lough Gur region commonly speak of the *Good People* or the *Kind People* or the *Little People*, their names for the fairies. The leprechaun indicates the place where hidden treasure is to be found. If the person to whom he reveals such a secret makes it known to a second person, the first person dies, or else no money is found: in some cases, the money is changed into ivy leaves or furze blossoms.

'I am convinced that some of the older peasants still believe in fairies. I used to go out on the lake occasionally on moonlight nights, and an old woman supposed to be a "wise woman" (a Seeress), hearing about my doing this, told me that under no circumstances should I continue the practice, for fear of "Them People" (the fairies). One evening in particular I was warned by her not to venture on the lake. She solemnly asserted that the" Powers of Darkness" were then abroad and that it would be a misfortune for me to be in their path. [2]

'Under ordinary circumstances, as a very close observer of the Lough Gur peasantry informs me, the old people will

pray to the Saints, but if by any chance such prayers remain unanswered, they then invoke other powers, the fairies, the goddesses Aine and Fennel, or other pagan deities, whom they seem to remember in a vague subconscious manner through tradition.'

TESTIMONY FROM A COUNTY KERRY SEER

To another of my fellow students in Oxford, a native Irishman of County Kerry, I am indebted for the following evidence:--

A Collective Vision of Spiritual Beings.--'Some few weeks before Christmas, 1910, at midnight on a very dark night, I and another young man (who like myself was then about twenty-three years of age) were on horseback on our way home from Limerick. When near Listowel, we noticed a light about half a mile ahead. At first, it seemed to be no more than a light in some house; but as we came nearer to it and it was passing out of our direct line of vision we saw that it was moving up and down, to and fro, diminishing to a spark, then expanding into a yellow luminous flame. Before we came to Listowel we noticed two lights, about one hundred yards to our right, resembling the light seen first. Suddenly each of these lights expanded into the same sort of yellow luminous flame, about six feet high by four feet broad. Amid each flame, we saw a radiant being having human form. Presently the lights moved toward one another and made contact, whereupon the two beings in them were seen to be walking side by side. The beings' bodies were formed of a pure dazzling radiance, white like the radiance of the sun, and much brighter than the yellow light or aura surrounding them. So dazzling was the radiance, like a halo, round their heads that we could not distinguish the countenances of the beings; we could only distinguish the general shape of their bodies; though their heads were very clearly outlined because this halo-like radiance, which was the brightest light about them, seemed to radiate from or rest upon the head of each being. As we travelled on; a house intervened between us and the lights, and we saw

no more of them. It was the first time we had ever seen such phenomena, and in our hurry to get home, we were not wise enough to stop and make further examinations. But ever since that night, I have frequently seen, both in Ireland and in England, similar lights with spiritual beings in them.' *The reality of the Spiritual World.--*' Like my companion, who saw all that I saw of the first three lights, I formerly had always been a sceptic as to the existence of spirits; now I know that there is a spiritual world. My brother, a physician, had been equally sceptical until he saw, near our home at Listowel, similar lights containing spiritual beings and was obliged to admit the genuineness of the phenomena,

'In whatever country we may be, I believe that we are forever immersed in the spiritual world; but most of us cannot perceive it on account of the unrefined nature of our physical bodies. Through meditation and psychical training one can come to see the spiritual world and its beings. We pass into the spirit realm at death and come back into the human world at birth; and we continue to reincarnate until we have overcome all earthly desires and mortal appetites. Then the higher life is open to our consciousness and we cease to be human; we become divine beings.' (Recorded in Oxford, England, August 12, 1911.)

The Clairvoyance of Mike Farrell.--'Mike Farrell, too, could tell all about the *gentry*, as he lay sick a long time. And he told about Father Brannan's youth, and even the house in Roscommon in which the Father was born; and Father Brannan never said anything more against Mike after that. Mike surely saw the *gentry*; and he was with them during his illness for twelve months. He said they live in *forts* and at Alt Darby ("the Big Rock"). After he got well, he went to America, at the time of the famine.'

The 'Gentry' Army.--' The *gentry* were believed to live up on this hill (Hill of the Brocket Stones, *Clutch-a-brace*), and from it, they would come out like an army and march along the road to the strand. Very few people could see them. They were thought to be like living people but in different dresses. They seemed like soldiers, yet it was known they were not living beings such as we are.'

The Seership of Dan Quinn.--' On Connor's Island (about two miles southward from Cairns by the mainland) my uncle,

Dan Quinn, often used to see big crowds of the *gentry* come into his house and play music and dance. The house would be full of them, but they caused him no fear. Once on such an occasion, one of them came up to him as he lay in bed, and giving him a green leaf told him to put it in his mouth. When he did this, instantly he could not see the *gentry*, but could still hear their music. Uncle Dan always believed he recognized in some of the *gentry* his drowned friends. Only when he was alone would the *gentry* visit him. He was a silent old man, and so never talked much; but I know that this story is as true as can be and that the *gentry* always took an interest in him.'

UNDER THE SHADOW OF BENBULBEN AND BEN WASKIN

I was driving along the BenBulbin road, on the ocean side, with Michael Oates, who was on his way from his mountain-side home to the lowlands to cut hay; and as we looked up at the ancient mountain, so mysterious and silent in the shadows and fog of a calm early morning of summer, he told me about its invisible inhabitants:--

The 'Gentry' Huntsmen.--'I knew a man who saw the *gentry* hunting on the other side of the mountain. He saw hounds and horsemen cross the road and jump the hedge in front of him, and it was one o'clock at night. The next day he passed the place again, and looked for the tracks of the huntsmen, but saw not a trace of tracks at all.'

The 'Taking' of the Turf-Cutter.--After I had heard about two boys who were drowned opposite Inishmurray, and who afterwards appeared as apparitions, for the *gentry* had them, this curious story was related:--'A man was cutting turf out on the side of Benbulben when a strange man came to him and said, "You have cut enough turf for to-day. You had better stop and go home." The turf-cutter looked around in surprise, and in two seconds the strange man had disappeared; but he decided to go home. And as soon as he was home, such a feeling came over him that he could not tell whether he was alive or dead. Then he took to his bed and never rose again.'

Hearing the 'Gentry' Music.--At this Michael said to his companion in the cart with us, William Barber, 'You tell how you heard the music'; and this followed:--'One night, about one o'clock, myself and another young man were passing along the road up there round Ben Bulbin when we heard the finest kind of music. All sorts of music seemed to be playing. We could see nothing at all, though we thought we heard voices like children's. It was the music of the *gentry* we heard.'

My next friend to testify is Pat Ruddy, eighty years old, one of the most intelligent and prosperous farmers living beside Ben Bulben. He greeted me in the true Irish way, but before we could come to talk about fairies his good wife induced me to enter another room where she had secretly prepared a great feast spread out on a fresh white cloth, while Pat and myself had been exchanging ols about America and Ireland. When I returned to the kitchen, the whole family was assembled around the blazing turf fire, and Pat was soon talking about the 'gentry." --

Seeing the 'Gentry' Army.--'Old people used to say the *gentry* were in the mountains; that is certain, but I never could be quite sure of it myself. One night, however, near midnight, I did have a sight: I set out from Bantrillick to come home, and near Ben Bulben there was the greatest army you ever saw, five or six thousand of them in armour shining in the moonlight. A strange man rose out of the hedge and stopped me, for a minute, in the middle of the road. He looked into my face, and then let me go.'

An Ossianic Fragment.--' A man went away with the *good people* (or *gentry*) and returned to find the townland all in ruins. As he came back riding on a horse of the *good people*, he saw some men in a quarry trying to move a big stone. He helped them with it, but his saddle girth broke, and he fell to the ground. The horse ran away, and he was left there, by an old man.

SCHOOLMASTER'S TESTIMONY

A schoolmaster, who is a native of the BenBulbin country, offers this testimony: --' There is an implicit belief here in the *gentry*, especially among the old people. They consider them the spirits of their departed relatives and friends, who visit them in joy and sorrow. On the death of a member of a family, they believe the spirits of their near relatives are present; they do not see them but feel their presence. They even have a strong belief that the spirits show them the future in dreams; and say that cases of affl, are always foreshown in a dream.

'The belief in changelings is not now generally prevalent; but in olden times a mother used to place a pair of iron tongs over the cradle before leaving the child alone, in order that the fairies should not change the child for a weak one of their own. It was another custom to take a wisp of straw and, lighting one end of it, make a fiery sign of the cross over a cradle before a baby could be placed in it.'

WITH THE IRISH MYSTICS IN THE *SIDHE* WORLD

Let us now turn to the Rosses Point country, which, as we have already said, is one of the very famous mountaintops for the' gentry', or, as educated Irish seers who make pilgrimages thither call them, the *Slake*. I have been told by more than one such seer that there on the hills and Greenlands (a great stretch of open country, treeless and grass-grown), and on the strand at Lower Rosses Point--called Wren Point by the country-folk--these beings country found their wonderful music heard; and a well-known Irish artist has shown me many drawings, and paintings in oil, of these *Sidhe* people as he has often beheld them at those

places and elsewhere in Ireland. They are described as a race of majestic appearance and marvellous beauty, in form human, yet in nature divine. The highest order of them seems to be a race of beings evolved to a superhuman plane of existence, such as the ancients called gods; and with this opinion, strange as it may seem in this age, all the educated Irish seers with whom I have been privileged to talk agree, though they go further, and say that these highest *Sidhe* races still inhabiting Ireland are the ever-young, immortal divine race known to the ancient men of Erin as the Tuatha De Danann.

Of all European lands, I venture to say that Ireland is the most mystical, and, in the eyes of true Irishmen, as much the Magic Island of Gods and Initiates now as it was when the Sacred Fires flashed from its purple, heather-covered mountain-tops and mysterious round towers, and the Greater Mysteries drew to its hallowed shrines neophytes from the West as well as from the East, from India and Egypt as well as from Atlantis; [1] and Erin's mystic-seeing sons still watch and wait for the relighting of the Fires and the restoration of the old Druidic Mysteries. Herein I but imperfectly echo the mystic message Ireland's seers gave me, a pilgrim to their Sacred Isle. And until this mystic message is interpreted, men cannot discover the secret of Gaelic myth and song in olden or in modern times, they cannot drink at the ever-flowing fountain of Gaelic genius, the perennial source of inspiration which lies behind the new revival of literature and art in Ireland, nor understand the seeming reality of the fairy races.

AN IRISH MYSTIC'S TESTIMONY

Through the kindness of an Irish mystic, who is a seer, I am enabled to present here, in the form of a dialogue, very rare and very important evidence, which will serve to illustrate and to confirm what has just been paid above about the mysticism of Ireland. To anthropologists, this evidence may be of more than ordinary value when they know that

it comes from one who is not only a cultured seer but who is also a man conspicuously successful in the practical life of a great city:--

Visions.--

Q.--Are all visions which you have had of the same character?

A.--'I have always made a distinction between pictures seen in the memory of nature and visions of actual beings now existing in the inner world. We can make the same distinction in our world: I may close my eyes and see you as a vivid picture in memory, or I may look at you with my physical eyes and see your actual image. In seeing these beings of which I speak, the physical eyes may be open or closed: mystical beings in their own world and nature are never seen with the physical eyes.'

Otherworlds.--

Q.--By the inner world do you mean the Celtic Otherworld?

A.--'Yes; though there are many Other Worlds. The *Tir-na-nog* of the ancient Irish, in which the races of the *Sidhe* exist, may be described as a radiant archetype of this world, though this definition does not at all express its psychic nature. In *Tir-na-nog* one sees nothing save harmony and beautiful forms. There are other worlds in which we can see horrible shapes.'

Classification of the 'Sidhe'.--

Q.--Do you in any way classify the *Sidhe* races to which you refer?

A.--'The beings whom I call the *Sidhe*, I divide, as I have seen them, into two great classes: those which are shining, and those which are opalescent and seem lit up by a light within themselves. The shining beings appear to be lower in the hierarchies; the opalescent beings are more rarely seen, and appear to hold the positions of great chiefs or princes among the tribes of Dana.'

Conditions of Seership.--

Q.--Under what state or condition and where have you seen such beings?

A.--'I have seen them most frequently after being away from a city or town for a few days. The whole west coast of Ireland from Donegal to Kerry seems charged with a magical power, and I find it easiest to see while I am there. I have always found it comparatively easy to see visions while at ancient monuments like NewGrange and Dowth, because I think such places are naturally charged with psychical forces, and were for that reason made use of long ago as sacred places. I usually find it possible to throw myself into the mood of seeing; but sometimes visions have forced themselves upon me.'

The Shining Beings.--

Q.--Can you describe the shining beings?

A.--'It is very difficult to give any intelligible description of them. The first time I saw them with great vividness I was lying on a hill-side alone in the west of Ireland, in County Sligo: I had been listening to music in the air, and to what seemed to be the sound of bells, and was trying to understand these aerial clashings in which wind seemed to break upon wind in an ever-changing musical silvery sound. Then the space before me grew luminous, and I began to see one beautiful being after another.'

The Opalescent Beings.--

Q.--Can you describe one of the opalescent beings?

A.--' The first of these I saw I remember very clearly, and the manner of its appearance: there was at first a dazzle of light, and then I saw that this came from the heart of a tall figure with a body shaped out of half-transparent or opalescent air, and throughout the body ran a radiant, electrical fire, to which the heart seemed the centre. Around the head of this being and through its waving luminous hair, which was blown all about the body like living strands of gold, there appeared flaming wing-like auras. From the being itself, light seemed to stream outwards in every direction; and the effect left on me after the vision was one of extraordinary lightness, joyousness, or ecstasy.

'At about this same period of my life, I saw many of these

great beings and I then thought that I had visions of Aengus, Manannan, Lug, and other famous kings or princes among the Tuatha De Danann; but since then I have seen so many beings of a similar character that I now no longer would attribute to any one of them personal identity with particular beings of legend; though I believe that they correspond in a general way to the Tuatha De Danann or ancient Irish gods.'

The stature of the 'Sidhe'.--

Q.--You speak of the opalescent beings as great beings; what stature do you assign to them, and the shining beings?

A.--'The opalescent beings seem to be about fourteen feet in stature, though I do not know why I attribute to them such definite height, since I had nothing to compare them with; but I have always considered them as much taller than our race. The shining beings seem to be about our own stature or just a little taller. Peasant and other Irish seers do not usually speak of the *Sidhe* as being little, but as being tall: an old schoolmaster in the West of Ireland described them to me from his own visions as tall beautiful people, and he used some Gaelic words, which I took as meaning that they were shining with every colour.'

The worlds of the 'Sidhe.'--

Q.--Do the two orders of *Sidhe* beings inhabit the same world?

A.--'The shining beings belong to the mid-world; while the opalescent beings belong to the heaven-world. There are three great worlds which we can see while we are still in the body: the earth-world, mid-world, and heaven-world.'

Nature of the 'Sidhe.'--

Q.--Do you consider the life and state of these *Sidhe* beings superior to the life and state of men?

A.--' I could never decide. One can say that they

are certainly more beautiful than men are, and that their worlds seem more beautiful than our world.

'Among the shining orders there does not seem to be any individualised life: thus if one of them raises his hands all raise their hands, and if one drinks from a fire-fountain all do; they seem to move and to have their real existence in a being higher than themselves, to which they are a kind of body. Theirs is, I think, a collective life, so individualised and so calm that I might have more varied thoughts in five hours than they would have in five years; and yet one feels an extraordinary purity and, exaltation about their life. Beauty of form with them has never been broken up by the passions which arise in the developed egotism of human beings. A hive of bees has been described as a single organism with disconnected cells; and some of these tribes of shining beings seem to be little more than one being manifesting itself in many beautiful forms. I speak this with reference to the shining beings only: I think that among the opalescent or *Sidhe* beings, in the heaven-world, there is an even closer spiritual unity, but also a greater individuality.'

Influence of the 'Sidhe' on Men.--

Q.--Do you consider any of these *Sidhe* beings inimical to humanity?

A.--'Certain kinds of the shining beings, whom I call wood beings, have never affected me with any evil influences I could recognize. But the water beings, also of the shining tribes, I always dread, because I felt whenever I came into contact with them a great drowsiness of mind and, I often thought, an actual drawing away of vitality.'

Water Beings Described.--

Q.--Can you describe one of these water beings?

A.--' In the world under the waters--under a lake in the West of Ireland in this case--I saw a blue and orange coloured king seated on a throne, and there seemed to be some fountain of mystical fire rising from under his throne, and he breathed this fire into himself as though it were his life. As I looked, I saw groups of pale beings, almost grey in colour, coming down one side of the throne by the fire fountain. They placed their head and lips near the heart of the elemental king, and, then, as they touched him, they shot upwards, plumed and radiant, and passed on the other side, as though they had received a new life from this chief of their world.'

Wood Beings Described.--

Q.--Can you describe one of the wood beings?

A.--'The wood beings I have seen most often are of a shining silvery colour with a tinge of blue or pale violet, and with dark purple-coloured hair.'

Reproduction and Immortality of the 'Sidhe'.--

Q.--Do you consider the races of the *Sidhe* able to reproduce their kind; and are they immortal?

A.--' The higher kinds seem capable of breathing forth beings out of themselves, but I do not understand how they do so. I have seen some of them who contain elemental beings within themselves, and these they could send out and receive back within themselves again.

'The immortality ascribed to them by the ancient Irish is only a relative immortality, their space of life being much greater than ours. In time, however, I believe that they grow old and then pass into new bodies just as men do, but whether by birth or by the growth of a new body I cannot say, since I have no certain knowledge about this.'

Sex among the 'Sidhe'--

Q.--Does sexual differentiation seem to prevail among the Sidhe races?

A.--'I have seen forms both male and female, and forms which did not suggest sex at all.'

'Sidhe' and Human Life.--

Q.--(1) is it possible, as the ancient Irish thought, that certain of the higher *Sidhe* beings have entered or could enter our plane of life by submitting to human birth? (2) On the other hand, do you consider it possible for men in trance or at death to enter the *Sidhe* world?

A.--(1) 'I cannot say.' 'Yes; both in trance and after death. I think any one who thought much of the *Sidhe* during his life and who saw them frequently and brooded on them would likely go to their world after death.'

Social Organization of the 'Sidhe'.--

Q.--You refer to chieftain-like or prince-like beings, and a king among water beings; is there therefore definite social organisation among the various *Sidhe* orders and races, and if so, what is its nature?

A.--' I cannot say about a definite social organisation. I have seen beings who seemed to command others, and who were held in reverence. This implies an organisation, but whether it is instinctive like that of a hive of bees, or consciously organised like human society, I cannot say.'

Lower 'Sidhe' as Nature Elementals.--

Q.--You speak of the water-being king as an elemental king; do you suggest thereby a resemblance between lower *Sidhe* orders and what mediaeval mystics called elementals?

A.--' The lower orders of the *Sidhe* are, I think, the natural elementals of the mediaeval mystics.'

Nourishment of the Higher 'Sidhe'.--

Q.--The water beings as you have described them seem to be nourished and kept alive by something akin to electrical fluids; do the higher orders of the *Sidhe* seem to be similarly nourished?

A.--' They seemed to me to draw their life out of the Soul of the World.'

Collective Visions of 'Sidhe' Beings.--

Q.--Have you had visions of the various *Sidhe* beings in company with other persons?

A.--' I have had such visions on several occasions.'

This statement has been confirmed to me by three participants in such collective visions, who separately at different times have seen in company with our witness the same vision at the same moment. On another occasion, on the Greenlands at Rosses Point, County Sligo, the same

Sidhe being was seen by our present witness and a friend with him, also possessing the faculty of seership, at a time when the two recipients were some little distance apart, and they hurried to each other to describe the being, not knowing that the explanation was mutually unnecessary. I have talked with both recipients so much, and know them so intimately that I am fully able to state that as recipients they fulfil all necessary pathological conditions required by psychologists to make their evidence acceptable.

PARALLEL EVIDENCE AS TO THE *SIDHE* RACES

In general, the rare evidence above recorded from the Irish seer could be paralleled by similar evidence from at least two other reliable Irish people, with whom also I have been privileged to discuss the Fairy Faith. One is a member of the Faithful Irish Academy, the other is the wife of a well-known Irish historian, and both of them testify to having likewise had collective visions of *Sidhe* beings in Ireland.

This is what Mr. William B. Yeats wrote to me, while this study was in progress, concerning the Celtic Fairy Kingdom:--' I am certain that it exists, and will someday be studied as it was studied by Kirk.'

INDEPENDENT EVIDENCE FROM THE *SIDHE* WORLD

One of the most remarkable discoveries of our Celtic research has been that the native population of the Rosses Point country, or, as we have called it, the *Sidhe* world, in most essentials, and, what is most important, by independent folk testimony, substantiate folk testimony and statements of the educated Irish mystics to whom we have just referred, as follows:--

John Conway's Vision of the 'Gentry'.--In Upper Rosses Point, Mrs. J. Conway told me this about the 'gentry':--' John Conway, my husband, who was a pilot by profession,

in watching for in-coming ships used to go up on the high hill among the Fairy Hills; and there he often saw the *gentry* going down the hill to the strand. One night in particular he recognized them as men and women of the *gentry* and they were as big as any living people. It was late at night about forty years ago.'

Ghosts and Fairies.--When first I introduced myself to Owen Conway, in his bachelor quarters, a cosy cottage at Upper Rosses Point, he said that Mr. W. B. Yeats and other men famous in Irish literature had visited him to hear about the fairies, and though he knew very little about the fairies he nevertheless always liked to talk of them. Then Owen began to tell me about a man's ghost which both he and Bran Reggan had seen at different times on the road to Sligo, then about a woman's ghost which he and other people had often seen near where we were, and then about the exercising of a haunted house in Sligo some sixty years ago by Father McGowan, who as a result died soon afterwards, apparently having been killed by the exorcised spirits. Finally, I heard from him the following anecdotes about the fairies:

A Stone Wall overthrew by 'Fairy' Agency.--' Nothing is more certain than that there are fairies. The old folks always thought them the fallen angels. At the back of this house, the fairies had their pass. My neighbour started to build a cow-shed, and one wall abutting on the pass was thrown down twice, and nothing but the fairies ever did it. The third time the wall was built it stood.'

Fairies passing through Stone Walls.--' Where MacEwen's house stands was a noted fairy place. Men in the building saw fairies on horses coming across the spot, and the stone walls did not stop them at all.'

Seeing the 'Gentry'.--' A cousin of mine, who was a pilot, once went to the watch-house up there on the Point to take his brother's place; and he saw ladies coming towards him as he crossed the Greenlands. At first, he thought they were coming from a dance, but there was no dance going on then, and, if there had been, no human beings dressed like them

and moving as they were could have come from any part of the globe, and in so great a party, at that hour of the night. Then when they passed him and he saw how beautiful they were, he knew them for the *gentry* women.'

'Michael Reddy (our next witness) saw the *gentry* down on the Greenlands in regimentals like an army, and in daylight. He was a young man at the time, and had been sent out to see if any cattle were astray.'

And this is what Michael Reddy, of Rosses Point, now a sailor on the ship *Tartar*, sailing from Sligo to neighbouring ports on the Irish coast, asserts in confirmation of Owen Conway's statement about him:--'I saw the *gentry* on the strand (at Lower Rosses Point) about forty years ago. It was afternoon. I first saw one of them like an officer pointing at me what seemed like a sword; and when I got on the Greenlands I saw a great company of *gentry*, like soldiers, in red, laughing and shouting. Their leader was a big man, and they were ordinary human size. As a result [of this vision] I took to my bed and lay there for weeks. On another occasion, late at night, I was with my mother milking cows, and we heard the *gentry* all around us talking, but could not see them.'

Going to the 'Gentry' through Death, Dreams, or Trance.--John Conway, one of the most reliable citizens of Upper Rosses Point, offers the following testimony concerning the 'gentry':--'In olden times the *gentry* were very numerous about *forts* and here on the Greenlands, but rarely seen. They appeared to be the same as any living man. When people died it was said the *gentry* took them, for they would afterwards appear among the *gentry*.'

"We had a ploughman of good habits who came in one day too late for his morning's work, and he very seriously said, "May be if you had travelled all night as much as I have you wouldn't talk. I was away with the *gentry*, and save for a lady I couldn't have been back now. I saw a long hall full of many people. Some of them I knew and some I did not know. The lady saved me by telling me to eat no food there, however enticing it might be.""

'A young man at Drumcliffe was *taken* [in a trance state], and was with the *Daoine Maithe* some time, and then got back. Another man, whom I knew well, was haunted by the *gentry* for a long time, and he often went off with *them* (apparently in a dream-themrance state).

'Sidhe' Music.--The story which now follows substantiates the testimony of cultured Irish seers that at Lower Rosses Point the music of the *Sidhe* can be heard:--'Three women were gathering shell-fish, in the month of March, on the lowest point of the strand (Lower Rosses or Wren Point) when they heard the most beautiful music. They set to work to dance with it, and danced themselves sick. They then thanked the invisible musician and went home.'

THE TESTIMONY OF A COLLEGE PROFESSOR

Our next witness is the Rev. Father--a professor in a Catholic college in West Ireland, most of his statements are based on events which happened among his acquaintances and relatives, and his deductions are the result of careful investigation:--

Apparitions from Fairyland.--'Some twenty to thirty years ago, on the borders of County Roscommon near County Sligo, according to the firm belief of one of my relatives, a sister of his was *taken* by the fairies on her wedding night, and she appeared there afterwards as an apparition. She seemed to want to speak, but her mother, who was in bed at the time, was thoroughly frightened and turned her face to the wall. The mother is convinced that she saw this apparition of her daughter, and my relative thinks she might have saved her.

'This same relative who gives it as his opinion that his sister was *taken* by the fairies, at a different time saw the apparition of another relative of mine who also, according to similar belief, had been *taken* by the fairies when only five years old. The child-apparition appeared beside its living sister one day while the sister was going from the yard into the house, and it followed her in. It is said the child was *taken* because she was such a good girl.'

Nature of the Belief in Fairies.--' As children, we were always afraid of fairies and were taught to say "God bless *them*! God bless *them*!" Whenever we hear them mentioned.'In our family, we always made it a point to have clean water in the house at night for the fairies.

EVIDENCE FROM LOUGH GUR, COUNTY LIMERICK

One of the most interesting parts of Ireland for the archaeologist and the folklorist alike is the territory immediately surrounding Lough Gur, County Limerick. Shut in for the most part from the outer world by a circle of low-lying hills on whose summits fairy goddesses yet dwell invisibly, this region, famous for its numerous and well-preserved cromlechs, dolmens, menhirs, and tumuli, and for the rare folk-traditions current among its peasantry, has long been popularly regarded as a sort of Otherworld preserve haunted by fairy beings, who dwell both in its waters and on its land.

There seems to be no reasonable doubt that in pre-Christian times the Lough Gur country was a very sacred spot, a mystic centre for pilgrimages and the celebration of Celtic religious rites, including those of initiation. The Lough is still enchanted, but once in seven years the spell passes off it, and it then appears like dry land to anyone fortunate anyone beholds it. At such a time of disenchantment, a Tree is seen growing up through the lake bottom--a Tree like the strange world tree of Scandinavian myth. The Tree is covered with a Green Cloth, and under it sits the lake's guardian, a woman knitting. [1] The peasantry about Lough Gur still believes that beneath its waters there is one of the chief entrances in Ireland to *Tir-na-nog*, the 'Land of Youth', the Fairy Realm. And when a child is stolen by the Munster fairies, 'Lough Gur is conjectured to be the place of its unearthly transmutation from the human to the fairy state.'

To Count John de Salis, of Balliol College, following legendary material, collected by him on the fairy-haunted Lough Gur estate, his ancestral home, and annotated by the Rev. J. F. Lynch, one of the best-informed antiquarians living in that part of South Ireland

The Fairy Goddesses, Aine--and Fennel (or Finnen).--' There are two hills near Lough Gur upon whose summit sacrifices and sacred rites used to be celebrated according to living tradition. One, about three miles southwest of the lake, is southwest Aine, Aine or Ane being the name of an ancient Irish goddess, derived from *a* "bright." The other, the highest hill on the lake-shores, is called Knock Luke shoresHill of the Goddess Fennel, from *Finnen* or *Finnine* or *Fininne*, a form of *fin*, "white." The peasantry of the region calls Aine one of the Good People; [1] and they say that

Fennel (her sister goddess or a variant of herself) lived on the top of Knock Fennel' (termed Finnen in a State Paper dated 1200).

The Fairy Boat-Race.--

'Different old peasants have told me that on clear calm moonlight nights in summer, fairy boats appear racing across Lough Gur. The boats come from the eastern side of the lake, and when they have arrived at Garrod Island, where the Desmond Castle lies in ruins, they vanish behind Knock Adoon. There are four of these phantom boats, and in each, there are two men rowing and a woman steering. No sound is heard, though the seer can see the weird silvery splash of the oars and the churning of the water at the bows of the boats as they shoot along. It is evident that they are racing, because one boat gets ahead of the others, and all the rowers can be seen straining at the oars. Boats and occupants seem to be transparent, and you

cannot see exactly what their nature is. One old peasant told me that it is the shining brightness of the clothes on the phantom rowers and on the women who steer which makes them visible.

'Another man, who is about forty years of age, and as far as I know of good habits, assures me that he also has seen this fairy boat-race, and that it can still be seen at the proper season.'

The Bean-Tighe. 'The *Bean-tighe*, the fairy housekeeper of the enchanted submerged castle of the Earl of Desmond, is supposed to appear sitting on art ancient earthen monument shaped like a great chair and hence called *Suidheachan,* the "Housekeeper's Little Seat," on Knock Adoon (Hill of the Fort), which juts out into the Lough. The *Bean-Tighe* as I have heard an old peasant tell the tale, was once asleep on her Seat when the *Buachaille* ₂ or "Little Herd Boy"

stole her golden comb. When the *Bean-Tighe* awoke and saw what had happened, she cast a curse upon the cattle of the *Buachailleen,* and soon all of them were dead, and then the "Little Herd Boy" himself died, but before his death, he ordered the golden comb to be cast into the Lough.'*Lough Gur Fairies in General.*--' The peasantry in the Lough Gur region commonly speak of the *Good People* or the *Kind People* or the *Little People*, their names for the fairies. The leprechaun indicates the place where hidden treasure is to be found. If the person to whom he reveals such a secret makes it known to a second person, the first person dies, or else no money is found: in some cases, the money is changed into ivy leaves or furze blossoms.

'I am convinced that some of the older peasants still believe in fairies. I used to go out on the lake occasionally on moonlight nights, and an old woman supposed to be a "wise woman" (a Seeress), hearing about my doing this, told me that under no circumstances should I continue the practice, for fear of "Them People" (the fairies). One evening in particular I was warned by her not to venture on the lake. She solemnly asserted that the" Powers of Darkness" were then abroad and that it would be a misfortune for me to be in their path.'Under ordinary circumstances, as a very close observer of the Lough Gur peasantry informs me, the old people will

pray to the Saints, but if by any chance such prayers remain unanswered, they then invoke other powers, the fairies, the goddesses Aine and Fennel, or other pagan deities, whom they seem to remember in a vague subconscious manner through tradition.'

TESTIMONY FROM A COUNTY KERRY SEER

A Collective Vision of Spiritual Beings.--'Some few weeks before Christmas, 1910, at midnight on a very dark night, I and another young man (who like myself was then about twenty-three years of age) were on horseback on our way home from Limerick. When near Listowel, we noticed a light about half a mile ahead. At first, it seemed to be no more than a light in some house; but as we came nearer to it and it was passing out of our direct line of vision we saw that it was moving up and down, to and fro, diminishing to a spark, then expanding into a yellow luminous flame. Before we came to Listowel we noticed two lights, about one hundred yards to our right, resembling the light seen first. Suddenly each of these lights expanded into the same sort of yellow luminous flame, about six feet high by four feet broad. Amid each flame, we saw a radiant being having human form. Presently the lights moved toward one another and made contact, whereupon the two beings in them were seen to be walking side by side. The beings' bodies were formed of a pure dazzling radiance, white like the radiance of the sun, and much brighter than the yellow light or aura surrounding them. So dazzling was the radiance, like a halo, round their heads that we could not distinguish the countenances of the beings; we could only distinguish the general shape of their bodies; though their heads were very clearly outlined because this halo-like radiance, which was the brightest light about them, seemed to radiate from or rest upon the head of each being. As we travelled on; a house intervened between us and the lights, and we saw

no more of them. It was the first time we had ever seen such phenomena, and in our hurry to get home we were not wise enough to stop an,d make further examination. But ever since that night I have frequently seen, both in Ir, eland and in England, similar lights with spiritual beings in them.' *The reality of the Spiritual World.*--' Like my companion, who saw all that I saw of the first three lights, I formerly had always been a sceptic as to the existence of spirits; now I know that there is a spiritual world. My brother, a physician, had been equally sceptical until he saw, near our home at Listowel, similar lights containing spiritual beings and was obliged to admit the genuineness of the phenomena,

'In whatever country we may be, I believe that we are forever immersed in the spiritual world; but most of us cannot perceive it on account of the unrefined nature of our physical bodies. Through meditation and psychical training one can come to see the spiritual world and its beings. We pass into the spirit realm at death and come back into the human world at birth; and we continue to reincarnate until we have overcome all earthly desires and mortal appetites. Then the higher life is open to our consciousness and we cease to be human; we become divine beings.' (Recorded in Oxford, England, August 12, 1911.)

which like the *Ka* is one of the many separable parts of the soul, is represented as a very little man with wings and a bird-like body. On Greek vases, the human soul is depicted as a pygmy issuing from the body through the mouth, and this conception existed among Romans and Teutons. Like their predecessors the Egyptians, the Greeks also often represented the soul as a small winged human figure, and Romans, in turn, imagined the soul as a pygmy with butterfly wings. These ideas reappear in mediaeval reliefs and pictures wherein the soul is shown as a child or little naked man going out of the dying person's mouth; and, according to Cædmon, who was educated by Celtic teachers, angels are small and beautiful -quite like good fairies.

Alchemical and Mystical Theory

In the positive doctrines of mediaeval alchemists and mystics, e.g. Paracelsus and the Rosicrucians, as well as their modern followers, the ancient metaphysical ideas of Egypt, Greece, and Rome find a new expression; and these doctrines raise the final problem--if there are any scientific grounds for believing in such pygmy nature-spirits as these remarkable thinkers of the Middle Ages claim to have studied as beings existing in nature. To some extent this interesting problem will be examined in our chapter entitled *Science and Fairies*; here we shall simply outline the metaphysical theory, adding the testimony of some of its living advocates to explain the smallness of elvish spirits and fairies.

These mediaeval metaphysicians, inheritors of pre-Platonic, Platonic, and neo-Platonic teachings, purposely obscured their doctrines under a covering of alchemical terms, to safeguard themselves against persecution, open discussion of occultism not being safe during the Middle Ages, as it was among the ancients and happily is now again in our generation. But they were quite scientific in their methods, for they divided all invisible beings into four distinct classes the Angels, who in character and function are parallel to the gods of the ancients, and equal to the Tuatha De Danann of the Irish, are the highest; below them are the Devils or Demons, who correspond to the fallen angels of Christianity; the third class includes all Elementals, sub-human Nature-Spirits, who are generally regarded as having pygmy stature, like the Greek daemons; and the fourth division comprises the Souls of the Dead, and the shades or ghosts of the dead.

For us, the third class, which includes spirits of pygmy-like form, is the most important in this present discussion. All its members are of four kinds, as they inhabit one of the four chief elements of nature. Those inhabiting the earth are called Gnomes. They are definitely of pygmy stature, and friendly to man, and in fairy lore ordinarily correspond to mine-haunting fairies or goblins, to pixies, *Corrigan*, leprechauns, and to such elves as live in rocks, caverns, or earth--an important consideration entirely overlooked by champions of the Pygmy Theory. Those inhabiting the air are called Sylphs. These Sylphs, commonly described as little spirits like pygmies in form, correspond to most of the fairies who are not of the Tuatha De Danann or 'gentry' type, and who as a race are beautiful and graceful.

Mystical Places.

Ireland's bones are made of stories, you can hardly step over a rock or walk past an old mound but if it could speak, it would tell you tales you could hardly imagine. But of all the legend glens and fields misty with memory in this ancient nation, there are few with as many secrets hidden in their depths as Lough Gur in county Limerick.

Situated between what we today call Herbertstown and Bruff, it is a lake in the shape of a dragon's mouth yawning wide, although it formed a perfect circle until it was drained for agricultural purposes in the 1840s, which exposed many of the treasures hiding below its waves.

In the middle of this once-circular lake is the hill of Knockadoon, upon which stands the Suideachan Bean-tí, the Housekeeper's Chair, also called Áine's birthing chair and the Old Hag's Chair, which is the seat of the fairy Áine, upon which no mortal may sit without losing their wits entirely!

Nearby can be found the largest Neolithic stone circle in Ireland, the Grange stone circle, also known as "Lios na Grainsi" or the "Stones of the Sun". These were used for rituals aligned with the summer solstice and were the site of great Aenachs, or festivals, where bonfires were lit and sporting events took place.

The lake is surrounded by great dolmens and pillars, ring forts, ruined castles, ancient farmsteads whose outlines can still be seen – the spectacles – and crannógs on their artificial islands, as well as a wedge tomb where once the bronze sickles of the druids shone wetly in the silvering moonlight.

People have lived here from the very earliest times, for six thousand years or more, and they hunted the giant elk whose bones still litter the area. It was said to have been sacred to Tuatha Áine, daughter of Dagda and brother of Fer Fi who once led the Tuatha. Her legend echoes even to this day, and she is known as the white lady, Bean Fhionn, or the lady of the house, Bean Tí.

Once every seven years she was said to summon a sacrifice to the lake and take them below to her country, as described by Mary Fogarty, born nearby in 1858:

"...some say that in ancient days there was a city where the lake is now before an earthquake threw up the hills and filled the hollow with water so that the city was submerged. Even now, the peasants say, when the surface of the lake is smooth one may see from a boat, far down and down again, the drowned city, its walls and castle, houses and church, perfect and intact, waiting for the Day of Resurrection.

And on Christmas Eve, a night without moon and stars, if one looks down and down again, one may see lights in the windows, and listening with the ears of the mind, hear the muffled chiming of church bells."

No poet or writer in Ireland will sleep on the shores of that lake, for fear of the visions they might have, or worse, that the lady might take too much of a liking to them! Such is told of the fate of Gearáid Iarla, the third Earl of Desmond, who helped to write the cruel Statutes of Kilkenny, intended to cause division and strife between the Norman invaders and the native Irish. For you see, the invaders were becoming more Irish than the Irish themselves!

He made it illegal to:

- Marry an Irish person
- Adopt an Irish child
- Use an Irish name
- Wear Irish clothes
- Speak the Irish language
- Play Irish music
- Listen to Irish story-tellers
- Play Irish games
- Let an Irish person join an English religious house
- Appoint any Irish clergyman to any church in the English settlement
- Ride a horse in Irish style, that is, without a saddle.

And if that wasn't enough, the man was reputed to be a black magician who sought to bind Sidhe Áine to his will and to be his mistress by stealing her cloak as she bathed under the starlight. Of course that was never going to end well, and despite his best precautions he was drawn into the lake to become one of the undead, only allowed to gallop wildly around the edge of the lake once every seven years.

The silver horseshoes by which he sought to flee in superstition are now the chain that binds him, for he can never return to the land of the living until they are worn away from the hooves of his horse entirely! Some say he will restore the House of Desmond when he is finished with his midnight rides, but you could be forgiven for doubting it.

Áine herself was said to have been the mistress of no less than Crom Cruach, or Crom Dubh, old black one-eye of the many glooms who was worshipped by some in Ireland in times past. And neither did they come to a good end, as with the Milesian King Tigernmas, who perished dreadfully in his dark festivities, along with most of his men!

The largest stone of the one hundred and thirteen Grange stone circle rears up more than four metres in height and is called Rannach Crom Dubh, or the division of Crom Dubh, and weighs more than forty tons.

Another manuscript tells a tale from the eighth century when Christianity was almost spread throughout the whole country – but not yet to every last corner! For a king of Munster whose name was Ailill Olom fell asleep on Cnoc Áine during the Samhain festivities, and found all the grass was gone from the hill when he opened his eyes!

Unable to explain this turn of events, he sought the counsel of a wandering seer, Fergus mac Comáin, who suggested they go back and see if it happened again. Well, the king fell asleep but the seer did not, instead hiding himself in the bushes so he was able to see the Sidhe King and Áine come forth from the hill!

The seer wasted no time but hopped out and murdered the Sidhe King, while Ailill Olom came awake and, unable to restrain himself, ravished Áine. In her fury at this assault she, in turn, ripped off his ear, and after that, he could no longer be king, for it was forbidden that any man should rule who was not whole in body.

Across from the hill of Knockadoon is another hill, called Knockfennel, which is also said to be hollow, although there is a small opening near the summit which grants access to any with the courage to enter the fairy otherworld. Fires were lit here on Samhain night, and six nights after the sick were brought out to be healed. If they were not healed by the ninth day of the moon they would hear the ceol Sidhe, the Suantraighe, ancient music Áine played to comfort those who were about to die.

Other stories tell of Bean and Tí sitting upon her throne, having come up from the lake, combing her hair with a beautiful golden comb. A shepherd boy watched from a distance, and when he saw that comb, he knew he had to have it for himself, so he crept up behind her and stole it while her attention was elsewhere!

After that, he had a terrible life filled with misfortune and failure, but before he died he ordered that the comb be thrown back into the lake, and so Áine got her comb back.

A poet-harper named Thomas O'Connell, who died during a feast at Bouchiers Castle around 1700 is buried nearby, and it was written:

.." in that churchyard by Lough Gur's romantic shore,
where the shamrocks and the ivy every grow
where the wild dove and the raven
like protecting spirits soar
o'er the green graves of silent Teampall Nua".

But perhaps strangest of all is the finding of the Lough Gur shield, or the sun-shield, which is a magnificent bronze age shield perhaps more than three thousand years old. It is one of a few of the same styles found as far abroad as Scotland and Denmark, which tells of a single people united in their ways and beliefs across all of the north and west.

It was, so they say, fished out of the lake with a gaff hook in 1872 by a young man called Cathal Hayes, who traded it to the historian Maurice Lenihan in Limerick for the price of a boat ticket to America. While he was there he kept the company of the Mayor of Boston, who married Josephine Hannon, whose father had been born at Lough Gur, and whose grandson became none other than US president John F Kennedy!

There is a tale, one of the oldest stories among the many very ancient stories of Ireland, of a man who returned to life as a man thousands of years after he first walked the earth.

His legend was found in an eleventh-century manuscript called Lebor na hUidre, which means The Book of Dun Cow, and it was written there by the followers of an early Christian Saint called Finnian of Moville.

The good Saint, centuries before, had recorded meeting a man who at that time went by the name of Tuan Mac Cairill, and who swore he had lived many lives and witnessed many deeds in Ireland. Finnian had travelled north upon hearing that there were yet people in Donegal who believed in pagan gods, and he had a mind to unmask these gods for what they were!

When he arrived he learned of a man, wise and hardy, who was claimed to be a magician and who observed neither the days of the Saints nor Sundays. Finnian was wroth and swore to educate this fellow and put his wisdom to the test, and stormed off to bang on the gates of this man's Dún, or fortress.

Finnian demanded entrance so that he could shine a light on the wickedness of the old ways and old gods, and banish forever their power over Ireland.

But the man within refused him and shuttered his doors and windows, continuing his ancient practices and blocking his ears to the rattling. He feared not the Saint for he feared not death nor time itself! He leapt over the scythe, he dodged under it, and the only occasion on which time laughs is when he chances upon Tuan, the son of Cairill, the son of Muredach Red-neck.

Well, I'll tell you, Finnian was seized with even greater wrath, but calling upon the power of God, he controlled himself and settled on a plan of action. He would sit outside the fortress and fast, praying loudly, until he was granted entry, relying on the idea that the occupant of the stronghold wouldn't sit idly by and let someone die famished on his doorstep, in defiance of the laws of hospitality.

The man inside thought about it carefully and decided that he'd wait until the Saint gave in and fled from hunger's gnawing at his wits, lifting the siege and leaving him in peace. But the mighty abbot wouldn't give in so easily, and he sat down on a spot just beyond the door. He bent his gaze on the ground between his feet and entered into a meditation from which he would only be released by admission or death

The man inside and his servants peered through spy holes day after day, hope slowly beginning to fade that this insistent visitor would take himself up and go elsewhere, but day after day the servants returned with the same message:

"The new druid is still there," they said.

As time passed, the servants grew more and more uneasy, for none were able to come or go from the place while this strange man sat outside. Oftentimes they would pace up and down and sometimes scream unexpectedly, for they felt mystic energies ebbing and flowing around them, pulling at their souls like implacable spiritual riptides.

"He has his own troubles," they said. "It is a combat of the gods that is taking place."

"If," said one irritable guard, "What if we buzzed a spear at the persistent stranger, or if one slung at him with a jagged pebble?"

"What!" his master demanded wrathfully, "is a spear to be thrown at an unarmed stranger? And from this house!" And he gave that man a clip on the ear. He rounded on the rest and told them to be still, and that the hunger would drive away the strange by the morning at the latest.

"Be at peace all of you," he said, "for hunger has a whip, and he will drive the stranger away in the night."

But the stranger didn't leave, and in the morning the lord of the house threw his hands in the air and gave up. The gate of the Dún swung wide and Finnian was carried inside, being unable to walk for hunger and exposure, but he was tough in body and mind and was quickly up and about.

Finnian had beaten the disease of Mugain, he had beaten his pupil the great Colmcille and he beat Tuan too, opening his heart as he had opened the gates of his home.

The two spoke long and long, and the master of the house, whose name was Tuan, learned much of the new faith. He wished to meditate upon this knowledge but the Saint insisted that Tuan speak of himself before they ate, over the objections of Tuan.

Tuan pleaded, "Let the past be content with itself, for man needs forgetfulness as well as memory."

But Finnian reminded him that deeds must be confessed before they can be forgiven, and sat until Tuan spoke, reciting his ancestors and family line, a matter of great importance in Ireland at that time. He quickly became confused however when Tuan started to recite two family trees, one more recent and one from very long ago – just after the flood!

Finnian pushed back his chair and leapt to his feet, his blood running cold as he looked upon his host with new eyes, but he could find no lie there. He then reached for the peace of God and found it, slowly seating himself again.

Tuan spoke on, relating tales of long-gone heroes as though he had shaken their hands only this morning. Of Partholon who some say first came to Ireland after the floodwaters receded he said was accompanied by forty-eight, half men and half women, the first to set foot in Ireland since the tall walls of ice marched implacably across the world, although who can say what came before?

A strange land they saw, one great forest from coast to coast, rich with birdsong beneath a warm and beautiful sun, and they built the first city there beside a roaring river. Fish and game aplenty were to be had, salmon pink, badgers, deer and rabbits, and more – strange, wild, shy monsters roamed freely, and shadows and spirits still haunting the world long after their bodies had drowned, creatures that you could see and walk through!

From those two dozen couples came no less than five thousand, although some say they were slow of wit, until over a day and night a dark wind blew from some hidden foetid place creaking wide beneath the earth, unleashing a dreadful plague which killed the whole race of Partholon – except one, Tuan himself.

Tuan fled, lost and terrified, into the endless forests, staring at the chirp of birds and the creak of trees, stalked by wolves and bears who sensed his weakness. He hid in a cleft rock, feared by nothing, for more than twenty years until he was more beast than man himself, and had forgotten much that men knew.

Then one day as he pawed through the dunes for shellfish to crack with a rock, he lifted his head to spy a fleet of thirty-four wide ships sailing towards the shore! Bright were their sails and fair their people, so he leapt for joy and followed the fleet along the coast like a goat, springing from rock to rock, until he stopped at a pool for a drink of water.

There he caught a glimpse of himself and was horrified to see his unkempt state and wild eyes looking back at him. He looked like neither man nor beast, with curved claws and withered, wrinkled skin, so he sat by the pool weeping for his loneliness and wildness, ashamed to make himself known and filled with sorrow for his life.

But a terrible storm arose and when he looked down from the tall clifftop he saw the fleet rolling and tossed by fierce waves. At times they were pitched against the sky and staggered aloft, spinning gustily there like wind-blown leaves.

Then they were hurled from these dizzy tops to the flat, moaning gulf, to the glassy, inky horror that swirled and twirled between ten waves. At times a wave leapt howling under a ship, and with a buffet dashed it into the air, and chased it upwards with thunder stroke on stroke, and followed again, close as a chasing wolf, trying with hammering on hammering to beat in the wide-wombed bottom and suck out the frightened lives through one black gape.

A wave fell on a ship and sank it with a thrust, stern as though a whole sky had tumbled at it, and the barque did not cease to go down until it crashed and sank in the sand at the bottom of the sea.

Impenetrable night drew a cloak over the ruin and horror of the children of Nemed, drawn by a vicious wind that strode the world long-legged, hiding all but the most piteous cries with its harsh whip cracks. Trees were pulled from the earth and leapt into the air, and the very boulders crashed down as though the land itself was trying to destroy the arrivals.

Tuan laid himself upon the earth then and slept, and in his dream, he became a great stag of the forests and felt the beating of a new heart within himself. When he awoke he found it was no dream, for he had in truth become that stag! Or perhaps his spirit passed into a lord of the woods.

Starin, fierce is the man,
I dread Scemel of the white shield,
Andind will not save me, though good and fair,
If it were Beoin

Though Biotech would leave me alive,
Cacher's rough fight is rough,
Britain achieves valour with his spears,
There is a fit of fury on Fergus.

They are coming towards me, O gentle Lord,
The offspring of Nemed, Agnoman's son,
Stoutly they are lying in wait for my blood,
To compass my first wound.

Then there grew upon my head
Two antlers with three score points,
So that I am rough and grey in shape
After my age has changed from feebleness.

He stood for a while tamping and breathing deep of the fresh air in amazement, tasting youth and savouring the sharpness of his new senses, until he smelled his deer kind and bellowed loudly with joy! He bounded light as a feather, launching himself ten metres at a spring, caressed by the gentled wind. None of his former tormentors would meet his eye, neither bear nor wolf could stand before him, and he reigned as king of the stags in Ireland.

Eventually, a time came when he smelled once again the scent of men, and he went to the north where he was Named and four couples had been saved from the wreck. He carefully drew near, knowing they would recognise him not, and saw them increase and multiply until four thousand couples lived and laughed and were riotous in the sun, for the people of Named had small minds but great activity. They were savage fighters and hunters.

And yet when he returned, to his grief he saw they were gone, the place that knew them and that they called home was silent, and only their bones glinted in the sun.

Age came upon him after that, and when his mighty head bowed for the last time, he returned to the cave he had lived in when he was an old man and was besieged by hungry wolves who swore he would be their next dinner. Proud yet, he agreed he would fight them on the morrow, knowing their tongue, and he lay down to sleep.

But as he slept he felt another change come upon him, and the long limbs of the stag became the sturdy legs of a boar with sharp tusks and a grisly gleam in his eye!

He heard the wolves call in mockery, and he answered with ferocity, tossing them up and reddening the loam with their blood, joyful in battle, a killer, a champion, a boar who could not be defied.

He took upon himself the lordship of all of the boars in Ireland, feared by hunting creatures and uncanny walkers in the wind both guardians of his tribes, sending even powerful bears fleeing with a whimper.

Only one creature did he not challenge, for men had once again returned to Ireland. Semion, the son of Stariath, with his people, from whom the men of Domnann and the Fir Bolg and the Galiuin are descended. These he did not chase, and when they chased him he fled, for no beast is ever truly a match for men.

Yet he often waited near to their settlements and listened, and remembered bitterly when his voice had been heard at the council table, and when the eyes of women would brighten to hear him sing. Little did he love his new life and his tusky herd when troubled by such happy memories.

A boar am I today among herds,
A mighty lord I am with great triumphs,
He has put me in wonderful grief,
The King of all, in many shapes.

In the morning when I was at Dun Bré,
Fighting against old seniors
The fair was my troop across the poor,
A beautiful host was following us.

My troop, they were swift
Among hosts in revenge,
They would throw my spears alternately
On the warriors of Fál on every side.

When we were in our gathering
Deciding the judgments of Partholon,
Sweet to all was what I said,
Those were the words of the true approach.

Sweet was my brilliant judgement
Among the women with beauty,
Stately was my fair chariot,
Sweet was my song across a dark road.

Swift was my step without straying
In battles at the onset,
Fair was my face, there was a day,
Though today I am a boar.

Time took its toll with the passing of many years, and he returned to his cave, awakening this time as a hawk. The lusty air was his kingdom, and his bright eye stared over every horizon. And still, he watched the doings of men far below.

He watched Beothach, the son of Iarbonel the Prophet, come to Ireland with his people, and there was a great battle between his men and the children of Simeon. Long he hung over that combat, seeing every spear that hurtled, every stone that whizzed from a sling, every sword that flashed up and down, and the endless glittering of the shields.

In the end, he saw that the victory was with Iarbonel. And from his people, the Tuatha Dé Danann and the Andé came, although their origin is forgotten and the unlearned believe them to be fairies and gods.

As a hawk, he sailed over the hills and mountains of Ireland, across her streams and rivers, over her lakes, and he knew the names of every tree and every glen under the sun or moon.

He was still a hawk when the sons of Míl, the Gaels, drove the Tuatha beneath the mounds with sharp iron and held Ireland as their kingdom against swords and witchcraft. It is from this age that the first lists of kings were written and the time of men truly began, the taming of Ireland.

But even the hawk with fierce joy in its heart grew old, and he returned to his cave to rest, where he fasted for three days and nights. Dreaming that the green tides of the ocean had arisen as before the coming of Partholon, he flailed in the waves and drowned, but did not die, for he awoke now as a salmon!

And this was a life he found much to his liking, for its purity and simplicity, for its unhindered passage through vast depths and up brawling rivers. Neither heat nor cold nor stumbling-roughness of the ground nor grasping winds troubled him here!

He was no king of all the salmon, leading multitudinous glittering shoals wherever he would, over green and purple distances beneath, through a world of amber and sparkling lucent blue. He arced like a living jewel through dusks of ebony shot with silver.

H saw the monsters of the uttermost ocean go heaving past, and the long lithe beasts that are toothed to their tails, and farther below, where gloom dipped down on gloom, vast, livid tangles that coiled and uncoiled, and lapsed down steps and hells of the sea where even the salmon could not go.

But then one day he remembered Ireland, and anguish returned to him, for he missed it sorely, and he felt fear then, knowing he must reach it or die forever!

It was a hard journey back for sickness had taken him, working its way through every muscle and bone in his body, and the soft waters seemed to have grown hard, but his unconquerable heart laboured onwards, until he reached the rich rivers and swam to the lakes, where he again saw men.

And they saw him too! They came to know him and look for him, lying in wait under waterfalls, holding out nets, but he was too wily for their hooks and strings and spears, although he took many a scar. All things seemed to hunt him then, the cat, the otter and the hawk until his life was an endless flight – and then he was caught!

The fisherman of Cairill, the King of Ulster, took him in his net, shouting for joy to see the size of his catch. He tried to flee and dive deep, tasting air like fire, but the fisherman told him to be still.

"Be at ease, O King," said the fisherman. "Be at rest. Let go of the stream. Let the oozy marge be forgotten, and the sandy bed where the shades dance all in green and gloom, and the brown flood sings along."

When the king's wife saw him she wished to eat him, and he was put over the fire and roasted, but his spirit passed from the salmon into her womb, and she gave birth to him as a son, prince of Ulster.

He forgot none of these things.

"And now," said Finnian, "you will be born again, for I shall baptise you into the family of the Living God!" And so it was done.

None know whether Tuan finally passed away into the arms of God in those distant ages when Finnian was still the Abbot of Moville, or whether he still keeps his fort in Ulster, or whether he climbed once again to his cave when the time came and now lives another life as another creature, seeing and remembering all things.

The Tuatha De Danann
By the force of potent spells and wicked magic,
And conjurations horrible to hear,
Could set the ministers of hell at work,
And raise a slaughtered army from the earth,
And make them live, breathe, and fight again.

So it was written in Keating's General History of Ireland, considered by many to be the definitive work bridging the Ireland of the ancient world with the Ireland of the modern world. He was working from texts we no longer possess and know only by reference, but there are still sections of the Lebor Gabála (the Book of Invasions, a very ancient tome) which tell of the occult necromantic skills of the Tuatha.

From the time before the flood, when the dread wizards recalled by Enoch walked the land when vast tablets of ice had buried half the world beneath gloomy fathoms of imponderable weight, when there were still dragons, wyrms steeped in wickedness, feasting on the nations of the earth, came the sorcery of the Tuatha Dé Danann.

The knowledge of these last vestiges of an elder age was passed on in secret to the druids of the Milesians when they came, especially the likes of Mogh Ruith who studied beneath the Sidh, in the dark underworld the Tuatha Dé Danann had retreated to. This added to the wisdom of the Fomorians brought forth from the grey-wracked ocean by rare travellers of that race, and became known across the realms for their power and wisdom.

Very often their rites and rituals centred around the head, where they believed the soul was seated. This was also reflected in cultures across the isles and the continent, with the Greeks recording that the Celts would have strings of severed heads hanging from the bridles of their horses. Later, they would be displayed around their homes, or embalmed in cedar oil and stored in a chest as war trophies. The Romans were also greatly disturbed by this habit, although they were not averse to taking a few heads themselves!

However, how the rich and varied tapestry of peoples who were later called the Celts took and preserved heads was quite different from the vengeful example-making of the Romans.

Noted was their habit of taking the heads of their most honoured friends and leaders, in some cases defleshing them and in others preserving them with oils and ointments, decorating them with jewels and golden plates, and keeping them in honoured positions of prominence. They might take the head of one of their allies in case it fell into the wrong hands. There may also have been a belief that you could influence a person's afterlife by the use of their head.

On the continent, temples have been found with niches for the most important heads to be placed, and human skulls were nailed over doorways and gates in farms and fortresses. Carven mouthless stone heads with closed eyes are found all over Ireland and Scotland, symbolising the dead.

Decorated skulls would have been used by the druids for drinking from their sacred springs and wells during their rituals, a tradition which is still spoken of – although not practised – near some holy wells in Ireland. This may also have been associated with the cult of Crom Cruach, which some have translated as "Ceann Cruaigh" or the bloody head.

Recent scientific examination has demonstrated that the cut and scrape marks created by the defleshing of the dead by Gaelic peoples are quite different from bones butchered for meat. Evidence for defleshing seems to go as far back as the mid-to Upper Palaeolithic, about 27,000 years ago, when individual skulls were heavily ochred and separately buried. This defleshing took place possibly after a period of excarnation, and before burial.

Cú Chulainn is said to have come back from his first battle with quite an array of severed heads, three attached to his chariot, nine in one hand and ten in the other, and no one was more impressed than his wife, Emer.

In the epic The Táin Bó Cualinge after cutting off twelve of his opponents' heads, Cú Chulainn planted twelve stones for them in the ground and set a head on each stone. In the story of Garb of Glen Rigel, Cú Chulainn met the two-headed Garb in single combat. He cut Garb's double head from his neck and impaled it with a stake.

But as strange and macabre as that might seem to us, it was nothing compared to what the heads used to do after being severed – for many are the tales that tell of heads continuing to speak, offering advice, giving orders, reciting poetry and more, long after being removed from their bodies!

Severed heads were valued for their association with divination and the supernatural, offering protection from malevolent spirits. Often enough a head taken in battle might be brought to a celebratory feast where food and drink were offered to it, and the turn head might tell a story. Sometimes heads didn't wait that long and would give orders on the battlefield where it had been slain.

These heads may have also served as gatekeepers and bridges into the Otherworld, transporting whole groups of people to strange places and times.

In the Táin the hero Sualtam is sent to awaken the men of Ulster to fight against invading forces, but in a freak accident, the sudden jumping of his horse causes his shield to slide, slicing his head clean off. His head continues to call for the Ulstermen's assistance, however, and it is this which finally brings them to the aid of Cú Chulainn.

In the story of the Destruction of Da Derga's Hostel, Conaire Mór, the famed king of Ireland, was attacked. After slaying many enemies, he asked his champion, Mac Cécht, to bring him some water. As the warrior returns with the drink, he sees two men lop off Conaire's head and, enraged, he kills them both. Conaire's head carries on talking, drinks the water, and composes a poem in honour of Mac Cécht's loyalty and prowess, which all things considered were impressive.

The head would thereafter speak when water from a sacred well was poured upon it.

In the Battle of Allen or the Cath Almaine, preserved in the 11th-century Yellow Book of Lecan, the men of Leinster fight against Fergal Mac Maile Duin, who is slain.

Fergal is beheaded and his head is taken to King Cathal who honours it, washes its braids and combs, smooths its hair, wraps a cloth of silk about it, and places seven oxen, seven wethers and seven cooked pigs before Fergal's head.

From the same book comes the tale of the Head of Donn Bó, a young man famed for his sweet singing who was slain at the battle and decapitated. Donn Bó had promised to sing that night for his lord Fergal no matter where they should be. One of the victorious called Baethge Lach went onto the battlefield to take a head back to the feasting place as a trophy.

As he approached, he heard the severed head entertaining the dead king's body on the field. The voice of Donn Bó was sweeter than the voice of any other head, or so the story goes. When the warrior approaches to lift his head, the head stops him and says it is pledged to sing for Fergal alone that night.

Nevertheless, he lifted the head, and taking it back to the building, placed it on a pillar. It is asked to sing, wherein it turned its face to the wall so that it was in darkness and sang so sweetly that all wept. It was finally taken back to the battlefield, where it was magically rejoined with its body.

A mighty warrior called Fothad Canainne never sat down to a feast without decapitated heads before him, and in turn, Mother's severed head sings a long poem to Ailill's wife after she lifts it.

Then there was Fothad Canainne, not the first man to lose his head over a woman but one of the few to tell about it afterwards! He was chieftain of the Connacht branch of the Fianna who fell in love with the wife of the leader of the Munster Fianna. They eloped, but her husband came after them with his men. Nearly all of them were killed in the ensuing scrap, and the poor woman, finding her lover's severed head, picked it up and carried it to where his body lay. Fothad's head then spoke to her, leaving her with a verse in memory of his life and tragic ending.

Fionn of the Fianna was not unfamiliar with talking conversational heads either, for when his favourite fool Lomna was killed upon witnessing his wife's adultery, Fionn found the headless body and followed it to the house of the murderer. Within there was none other than Lomas head beside the fire, but when the murderer Coirpre doesn't feed it any fish three times, Lomas head decides to tell the whole tale, but in riddles. So much did it talk that Coirpre eventually had to put it outside like a misbehaving dog, where it still refused to shut up!

There are many more such tales in Welsh and Scottish folklore, and even in pre-Roman British legends, such as The Assembly of the Wondrous Head where King Bran, having been mortally wounded in the foot with a poisoned spear, ordered his head to be cut off by his men. The head kept talking and was as good company as it ever was until it was buried.

And even more can be found, including the making of brain-balls of lime and... the brains of enemies... to be cast from slings. One such, called the Tathlum, was used by the Dé Danann lord Lugh to slay Balor of the evil eye, and the recipe for this is given as follows:

A tantalum, heavy, fiery, firm,
Which the Tuatha Dé Danann had with them,
It was that broke the fierce Balor's eye,
Of old, in the battle of the great armies.

The blood of toads and furious bears,
And the blood of the noble lion,
The brood of vipers and Osmuinn's trunks
It was of these the tantalum was composed.

The sand of the swift Armorian sea,
And the sand of the teeming Red Sea

*All these, being first purified, were used
In the composition of the tantalum.*

*Brian, the son of Bethar, no mean warrior,
Who on the ocean's eastern border reigned
It was he that fused, and smoothly formed,
It was he who fashioned the tantalum.*

*To the hero, Lugh was given
This concrete ball, no soft missile
In Mag Tuireadh of shrieking wails,
From his hand, he threw the tantalum.*

Peculiar tales persist about these traditional beliefs lasting even into recent times, such as that of a young man who travelled to Antrim in the 1940s for work. When there, he fell ill, but before he died asked that his friend cut off his head and carry it to his home village, where it can be buried with his people.

The friend duly returned the severed head to its home village, and the rest of the story tells how, as the funeral procession is approaching the graveyard, they saw another procession coming and – as was the custom, the story says – the funeral parties raced to see which would have the honour of holding their ceremony first. The other party won but, as it reached the graveyard wall, it vanished.

And then of course we have the Irish custom of carving turnips into heads, and even letting them dry year after year to give them a more wizened and wrinkled appearance, to be lit with candles on Hallowe'en, the time of the dead!

A Tragic Beauty.

Her name was Cliona or Clíodhna and she was one of the most beautiful women of the Tuatha Dé Danann, that vanished sorcerous race whose legends echo still from one end of Ireland to the other. Some even say she was the most beautiful woman in the world, and she was worshipped as a goddess by the pagans of Ireland who followed the fall of the Tuatha.

She was one of three daughters of Gebann, the chief druid of the sea-god Manannán Mac Lir, who had a particular fondness for her, much to her detriment, and was known for guarding against blighted crops and protecting animals, particularly cattle, from disease and from the evil eye. She was reputed to be able to change into a wren, as she did to escape one young mortal who had learned her magic, or a white hare.

She had three birds which ate from the fruit of a magical apple tree growing in Tír na nÓg, the Land of the Young, Tír Tairngire, the Land of Promise, and Magh Meall, the Pleasant Plain. Their bright song could sing anyone into a deep sleep which would heal all wounds, illnesses and injuries.

Together with Aoibhell and Áine she was one of the three goddesses of Munster. She had a great rivalry with Aoibhell and both of the women fell in love with a young chieftain called O'Caoimh. His fancy was for Aoibhell though, and they were engaged to be married. Cliona called on the help of an old wise woman skilled in dark and twisting arts, and Aoibhell began to fade away.

Cliona told her she'd be cured if she renounced the love of O'Caoimh, but Aoibhell refused, so Cliona gave her a lash of a magic wand which turned her into a white cat. Later O'Caoimh, not knowing where his bride to be had vanished off to, agreed to marry Cliona, but the old wise woman confessed to her part in the crime, and gave him the wand to turn the cat back into a woman.

It was Cliona's turn to spend some time as a cat then, for when he heard the full story he tapped her with it and regained his bride in the next stroke!

She had many titles, among them Queen of the Banshees, for it was said she ruled those spirits who sent up a bone-chilling wail before a death among one of the ancient families of Ireland. These were the sidheag, the fairy women of the hills, of South Munster, known as Cork and Kerry today.

Cliona would travel from her palace beneath Carraig Clíodhna, Clíona's Rock, or send forth one of her sister-subjects when the shadow of death stretched its hand over the descendants of those who had worshipped her. It was said there was no morning of the year when Clíona wasn't outside of that Carraig before sunrise, combing her long hair.

She was especially associated with the McCarthys, FitzGeralds, O'Donovans, O'Collins, O'Keeffes and O'Learys, but in particular the O'Donovans who came south from Uí-Fidghente before Saint Patrick landed, abandoning their worship of the goddess Mongfind for the love of Clíona. In later times, Domhnall Ó Donnabháin was referred to as the "Dragon of Clíodhna".

Domhnall's son, dragon of Cliodhna, is guardian of the ancestral name,
he will remit his authority to none other - he has accepted the law of his dynasty.

O'Donovan, Four Masters, vol. V, p. 1548

Clíodhna's Rock, anglicised as Carrigcleena, is a couple of hour's walk southwest of Mallow in the parish of Kilshannig, and the nearby stone circle has a reputation as a "door to the Otherworld" where Clíona betimes leads her fairy women in slow dances under the waxing moon. Another rock, Carrigcleenamore, off Inch Strand, two miles south and east of Rosscarbery, is known by locals as the seat of this goddess and path to the underworld.

Her palace plays a central part in a story about a man called Seán Mac Séamas, an Irish prince. Bewitched by a beautiful stranger he met during a feast at his father's hall, he bit a piece of apple she gave him before falling into a swoon.

Clíona took his prostate figure and carried him away to the rock, trapping him within and inside the otherworld. In desperation he wrote a letter in blood, slipping it out of a crack and into the whipping wind, which carried it to a cowherd. Once the king heard about this, he sought the help of a wise woman, who went to the rock, and, waiting until Clíona was brushing her hair in the morning, grabbed a handful and twisted it painfully it in such a way that Clíona could not look at her, since her mother warned

"If she lays her eyes on you, you're finished!"

She refused to release Clíona until the young prince was freed, and so it was done.

She was also said to lure young men to their doom in the watery grave which claimed her mortal form – for she left the safety of her fairy country to pursue a young man called Ciabhán of the curling locks, but Manannán Mac Lir grew jealous! So while her lover was away hunting, she rested her head on the strand Trá Théite at Cuan Dor or Glandore, the Harbour of the Oak Trees, between Skibbereen and Clonakilty.

Treacherous Manannán sent his mystical bard Iuchna to play magical music which put her into a far deeper sleep, and then she was drowned by a great wave! She swore a prophecy thereafter, that one day all of Munster would be swallowed by a terrible wave. And to this very day, every ninth wave, the strongest, or any particularly loud wave in the area is called "Tonn Clíona", or Clíona's Tide.

Fishermen in Cork still think it's bad luck to see a woman on the shore before you set out to sea.

Nor was her power forgotten until long after the Christianisation of Ireland! It was Fat Cormac McCarthy who ran into legal trouble while building his castle at Blarney in the fifteenth century, and he beseeched the ancient power for help.

She appeared to him, kissed his lips, and told him to kiss the first stone he found in the morning on his way to court. As a result, he pleaded his case with great eloquence and won, finishing his castle shortly after that. Thus the Blarney Stone is said to grant "the ability to deceive without offending", and Cormac was so pleased that he had the stone built into the wall at Blarney Castle, where countless numbers people visit every year to kiss the stone and get Clíona's gift for themselves.

So powerful were its effects that even Queen Elizabeth said in frustration that she could not complete a negotiation with Cormac MacCarthy and get her hands on his seat at Blarney Castle, since everything he said was "Blarney, as what he says he does not mean"!

Some stories about Clíona show her as dark and sinister, a dangerous and fatal figure, while others speak of her love and kindness, which may be why she remains so fascinating to this day. Among those who took a special interest in her was Irish revolutionary Michael Collins, who heard about her in the Rosscarbery school he attended and they took Sunday trips to Clíodhna's rock. Here, according to Michael's friend Piaras Béaslaí

Michael heard many wonderful tales of Clíodhna's enchantments, of wrecks and perils, and drownings and treasure troves.

Collins was descended from the Ó Coileáins of Uí Chonaill Gabra. Both the Uí Chonaill and the Uí Donnobhans were tribes within the Uí-Fidgety, and some have wondered whether that great son of Ireland heard the mournful song of the banshee before his fateful last day!

One midsummer's eve, when the Bel-fires were lighted,
And the bagpiper's tone called the maidens delighted,
I joined a gay group by the Araglin's Water,
And danced till dawn with O'Donovan's Daughter.

Have you seen the ripe monad and glisten in Kerry,
Have you marked on the Galtees the black whortleberry,
Or wave by the wells of Blackwater?
They're the cheek, eye, and neck of O'Donovan's Daughter.

Have you seen a gay kindling on Claragh's Round Mountain,
The swan's arching glory on Sheeling's blue fountain,
Heard a weird woman chant what the fairy choir taught her?
They have the step, grace, and tone of O'Donovan's Daughter!

Have you marked in its flight the black wing of the raven,
The rosebuds that breathe in the summer breeze waves,
The pearls that lie hidden under Lene's magic water?
They're the teeth, lips, and hair of O'Donovan's Daughter!

Ere the Bel-fire was dimmed or the dancers departed,
I taught her a song of some maid broken-hearted:

*And that group, and that dance, and that love song I taught her
Haunt my slumbers at night with O'Donovan's Daughter.*

*God grant, 'tis no fay from Cnoc-Firinn that woos me,
God grant, 'tis not Cliodhna the queen that pursues me,
That my soul lost and loan has no witchery wrought her,
While I dream of dark groves and O'Donovan's Daughter.*

*If, spell-bound, I pine with an airy disorder,
Saint Gobnait has sway over Musgry's wide border;
She'll scare from my couch when with prayer I've besought her.
That bright airy sprite like O'Donovan's Daughter.*

A Retelling

Long ago, in the time of the Tuatha Dé Dannan, one of their number became the high king of all Ireland, and his name was Eochaid Ollathair. He was a powerful magician of that sorcerous race, and by his workings he could change the weather and ensure the harvest was plentiful, as well as many other things.

His wealth was vast and he was much beloved by his people, but for all that he wasn't the happiest, for his eye had fallen on the wife of one of his subjects, Elcmar, whose name was Etain. And she herself was not unwilling, except for the considerable power of her husband. Fair as the first snow and lovely as a breath of wind across a calm sea, he was smitten and desired to have her, and in doing so caused events that would have been best left undone.

Eochaid hatched a scheme, coming up with an excuse to send Elcmar on a journey to a nearby Dún and return with tidings, but he cast powerful spells upon him before he left, such that night and day became one and he felt neither hunger nor thirst.

And while Elcmar wandered obviously in the wilderness for months on end, Eochaid came to Etain and they lay together, and she bore him a son, whose name was Aengus. So long was El Mar bespelled that she was fully over it by the time he returned, believing himself only gone a day, and Eochaid had spirited away the babe to the house of Midir to be raised.

Midir's house was in Tethba, a strange and magical part of the country, for he was one of the lords of the Sidhe, the people of the mounds, whose numbers were not known. Yet still, Eochaid was a powerful worker of wonders, and so the boy was accepted among thrice fifty youths who played ball all day long, and thrice fifty fair maidens who sang and danced.

There he was also called the Mac Óg, which means, the son of youth, for how else were they to call one who had been conceived at sunrise and born before sunset?

Aengus was raised there for nine years, in that uncanny place, and Midir told him that he was his own son, and so he treated him. He was marvellously swift of limb and strong of back, swift of mind and fair of face. But the other youths disliked his airs and swagger, for they knew themselves fosterlings, and further, they knew he was too.

One day a Fir Bolg called Triath made some rash comment to Aengus, and Aengus responded that it would be better for a peasant to address him with a little more respect!

"Would it indeed?" said Triath, "better yet if you knew who your parents were to begin with!"

And Aengus ran weeping to Midir and asked what this meant.

"No great problem," said Midir calmly, "for your father was Eochaid who is high king over all Ireland, and your mother was Etain, she of great beauty, and wife of Elmar. I raised you here, for knowing of your existence would cause him pain without end."

Well nothing would do for Aengus but that he be taken to meet his true father and ask of him lands for himself, as far away from the tongues of the Fir Bolg as he could get! And Midir agreed, so they travelled to meet Eochaid in Uisneach of Meath, the heart of Ireland, that was close by Tara and many other marvellous places of the ancient world.

The three met and clasped one another, and Eochaid asked Midir what this visit meant.

"He wishes to be acknowledged by his father, and lands given to him, for it does not seem right that the son of the King of Ireland should be landless!" said Midir.

Eochaid agreed but rubbed his forehead as a man with trouble on his mind.

"Happy I am to give him the land, but there is one problem – it is already occupied!" He said, "for it is the land of Elmar, and I have no wish to annoy him further, although it is the best land around, the Brú na Boinne."

So the three held council as to how they would overcome this problem, until Eochaid the crafty said to his son, "Wait until the Samhain, for on that day all men are at peace and on good terms with one another – then go to the Brú armed with a sword, for Elcmar will have nothing but his gold-brooch cloak and a forked hazel stick as he watches the youths playing. Then threaten his life, only sparing it if he allows you to be king of the Brú for a day and a night!"

"But what good will that do?" said Aengus.

"When he demands his lands back, you call upon my judgement as High King, and I will say that it is in days and nights that the world is spent, and the Brú is yours."

And so Aengus set out on the following Samhain, and threatened El Mar, who in return for his life, agreed to let Aengus be King of the Brú for a day and a night. After that time had passed however, he returned and demanded his lands back with savage threats and fury, and why would he not! But Aengus refused, and said instead that their case should be heard before Eochaid and all the men of Ireland.

To this Elcmar could hardly disagree, so they made their way to the High King, and put their arguments to him. Eochaid passed his judgement as he had said he would.

"So then this land accordingly belongs henceforth to this youth," said Elcmar.

"It is fitting," said Eochaid *"You were taken unawares on a day of peace and amity. You gave your land for mercy shown to you, for your life was dearer to you than your land, yet you shall have land from me that will be no less profitable to you than the Brú."*

He then granted Elcmar Cleitech, that was three of the lands about the Brú, and the fruits of the Boyne as well, and Elcmar was pleased enough with the agreement, so he went to his new home and made a strong place there.

A year to the day later Midir came back to visit Aengus, and found him watching a great sporting match between two groups of youths, with Elmar on his own mound in Cleantech, watching the same match. It *happened that a brawl broke out between the two sides, but Midir held back Aengus from intervening.*

"Stay right where you are," he said, "for if Elcmar decides to come down too, it might end very badly. I'll straighten this out!" and so saying, he went down among the young men and with some difficulty broke up the fight, although by mischance a split of holly caught him in the eye and what did it do but pop out of his head!

He came back to Aengus and held out his hand with the eye in it still, and great sorrow was on him.

"Oh I wish I'd never come for a visit, now look, I can't see the land I visit nor return to the land from whence I came!" wailed Midir, him being a king himself he must need to be whole in body and mind or his own people would reject him.

"Not a bit of it," said Aengus, "we shall visit Dian Cecht and he will set that eye back in your head!" and so that great healer of the Tuatha did.

"You must stay longer, even a whole year, so that you can see all of my lands and my hosts, my household and my herd," said Aengus, but it was the custom of those times to give to a guest whatever they might wish, as long as it could be done, by the ancient laws of hospitality.

So Midir asked for his guest-price, and that was "a chariot worth seven female slaves, clothes more fitted to my station, and the fairest maiden in all of Ireland."

"I have all of those except one," said Aengus, "who might be the fairest maiden in Ireland?"

"She is a princess called Etain," said Midir, "daughter of Ailill to the north and east, and by my pools and stones in all my long years I have never seen such beauty, such grace and such sweetness."

Well Aengus travelled to the house of Ailill in Moy n'Inis, where he was made welcome and stayed for three nights. He then announced who he was, where he'd come from, and what he was after.

Ailill was unimpressed, knowing well that he'd have no control over Aengus given the power of his father, and he told Aengus that if he shamed his daughter, there'd be no saving him. Aengus then asked the bride-price that would make her his own.

"No hard matter," said Ailill, "clear the forests and scrub from the twelve plains that are in my land, so that they might be settled for assemblies, strongholds, games and habitation, tilled and pastured."

"It shall be done!" gulped Aengus, and he left that place to go back to his father Eochaid, High King of Ireland. Eochaid sent his men and they cleared the twelve plains in a single day.

"Well done!" said Ailill, "but not yet done – for now I would like you to draw out from this land twelve great rivers from the bogs and moors, so that we may have fish from the sea and dry land where once there was swamp!"

"That's... fine!" said Aengus with a cheer he did not truly feel, and back he went again to Eochaid.

With a sigh the king sent not his men this time, but his wondrous powers of sorcery, and bent the bogs and marshes into twelve rivers, large and small, which flowed to the sea, and Etain's people profited greatly by them, but still Ailill's appetite was not satiated.

When Aengus returned to claim his prize, Ailill halted him with a word.

"First," said he, "you must leave the maiden's weight in gold and silver, for that is my portion of their price, all else goes to enrich her own people."

This at least Aengus needed no help with, and soon he had the gold and silver piled upon the floor to the weight of Etain and more. With that, they bade farewell to the hungry halls of the maiden's weight in gold and silver, and returned to Midir, who was already seated in his new chariot, wearing his new finery. Well pleased he was with that, and even better pleased with Etain, and she with him, and so they lay together.

A year and a day he stayed, but as he made ready to leave, Aengus pulled him aside to whisper words of warning.

"Best to keep an eye on the fair Etain, for the woman you married and who awaits your return, Fuamnach, has a fierce cunning and much knowledge and skill! She was raised by the druid Bresal Etarlam until you married her, and few are the arcane arts she does not know."

Well naughty old Midir went back to his strange realm, and there Fuamnach greeted him and made him welcome. Fuamnach offered to show the two around and see the places they had not yet visited, coming at last to their house. Etain went before them into the bedchamber, and Fuamnach told her to sit down.

"The seat of a good woman you have come into!" she hisses, and strikes her with a scarlet rod cut from a quicken tree, turning her into a pool of water!

Fuamnach fled to her foster father, the druid Bresal, and Midir could not stay in the flooded house, so he left without wife or consort.

In the summer's heat and with the wind blowing through the open windows and doors, the seething of the ground shrank the pool over time, so all that was left was a caterpillar, which turned into a beautiful purple butterfly.

She was as big as a man's head, the comeliest in the land, sweeter than pipes and harps and horns was the sound of her voice and the hum of her wings. Her eyes would shine like precious stones in the dark, and the fragrance and the bloom of her would turn away hunger and thirst from any she touched. The spray of the drops she shed from her wings would cure all sickness and disease and plague in anyone she passed. To listen to her and gaze upon her would nourish hosts in gatherings and assemblies in camps.

Midir only had to take one look at this magnificent creature and he knew it was his Etain, and as long as she stayed near he never took another wife or lover. He fell asleep to the sound of her gentle humming, and if enemies approached, she would awaken him.

But of course Fuamnach, the spurned wife, was not yet done wrecking her revenge, for ever higher did the fires of jealousy and hate burn in her heart!

Fuamnach decided one day to visit Midir, but before doing so she wrapped herself in strong walls of enchantment, the promises of the powers of the Dana - Lug, the Dagda, and Ogma.

Midir was enraged to see her coming, and he swore and cursed like a lunatic, telling her she wouldn't leave the place alive, but not a finger did he dare lift against her for fear of the powers that protected her.

Fuamnach sneered and said she regretted nothing, for it was better to look after herself than others, and if she came across Etain anywhere in Ireland, she'd do her terrible harm, whatever shape she hid in, for such was the wrath and terrible power of the Tuatha of old.

But crafty Fuamnach had heard and knew well of Midir's new friend, the purple butterfly, and quick enough she guessed that it was none other than Etain! She knew that whenever he saw the great butterfly, Midir loved no other woman, and found no pleasure in music or in drinking or eating when he did not see her and hear her music and voice.

Calling on the dark and unseen children of old night, Fuamnach summoned a fierce wind of assault and magic, hot with infernal fires, forcing Etain to flutter far from Midir. For seven years she could not find a summit or a tree or a hill or a height in Ireland on which she could settle, but only rocks of the sea and the ocean waves, until at last she landed exhausted on the cloak of Aengus.

His keen eyes saw well enough, and his ears had heard of this magical creature, so he said

"I bid you welcome, Etain, tired and weary wanderer, worn down with care and loss, you have met the wrath of Fuamnach! And after all I did to win you for Midir, now it seems like an idle task, for it has ruined you."

Aengus gathered her into the fleece of his cloak, and brought her to his home in the Brú, where he left her in his sun lantern, with crystal windows, wide for passing in and out of. He carried it with him wherever he went, and even when he slept it was by his side. He comforted and fed her fragrant and wondrous herbs, until her brightness and colour returned, thriving on their precious fragrance.

And yet Fuamnach heard of even this, and her heart was curdled with bitterness and fury. Concealing her bile, she went to Midir.

"Send for Aengus," she said "I would make peace between us at last, and I repent of my fury."

But when Midir sent a messenger to Aengus, she crept out not far behind, and circled round the Brú, entering by her eldritch arts. Finding the butterfly that was Etain, she again unleashed the same hell-wind, and it carried her out of the sun lantern and back upon the high and merciless winds.

In misery and weakness she fluttered along the blast of wind until she lit at last upon the rooftree of a house to the far north, where a feast was taking place, and from there she fell into the golden goblet that stood on the table before the wife of Etar the champion.

She was swallowed whole in one great and merry gulp, and that is how she came to be conceived again as a human being, and was born to that house, known as Etain, daughter of Etar.

By now, it had been a thousand and twelve years from the first begetting of Etain by Ailill until her last begetting by Etar, for the people of the tribe of Dana lived long and long, and counted little the passing of the years. And even today, among those with a trace of their blood, upon them age lies but a light hand.

Etain was raised as the champion's true daughter among the fifty daughters of other chieftains. It happened that one day they were bathing in the shallow waters of the northern sea when they saw a tall horseman riding towards them. His broad brown steed pranced and cantered, and curly was its tail and mane.

In red and green he was clad, and armoured about in silver and gold, with a great silver shield of an old sort. A five-pronged gold-banded spear was in his hand, and bright blond hair was held back by a golden ring about his head. He halted a while nearby and they gazed on his splendour with awe and fascination, when he uttered this lay:

> *This is Etain here today*
> *at Sid Ban Find west of Ailbe,*
> *among little boys is she*
> *on the brink of Inner Cichmaine.*
>
> *She it is who healed the King's eye*
> *from the well of Loch Da Lig:*
> *she it is that was swallowed in a drink*
> *from a beaker by Etar's wife.*
>
> *Because of her, the King shall chase*
> *the birds from Tethba,*
> *and drown his two steeds*
> *in the pool of Loch Da Airbrech.*
>
> *Full many a war shall be*
> *on Eochaid of Meath because of you:*
> *there shall be the destruction of elf mounds,*
> *and battle against many thousands.*
>
> *'Tis she that was sung of in the land;*
> *'tis she that strives to win the King;*
> *'tis she the Fair,*
> *She is our Etain afterwards.*

Then he rode off, and nobody knew where he had gone, and even less where he came from.

Well, you can imagine the rage felt by Aengus when he arrived at Midir's sidh and found no Fuamnach! Knowing well that he had been played false, and that if Fuamnach came across her there would be no mercy shown, he wheeled his horse about and rode as quick as he could back to the Brú.

He came into his house to see the sun lantern's crystal shattered upon the ground, and Etain long gone. Scouring about in red wrath, he found Fuamnach's track, and followed her back to the house of the druid Bresal Eterlam. There a ferocious but brief battle ensued, and the both of them were consumed by the fires of Manannan, perhaps caused by a spell cast wrongly, or the wrath of the powers of the Dannan at their conflict.

For so it was written:

> *Fuamnach the foolish one was Midir's wife,*
> *Sigmall, a hill with ancient trees,*
> *in Bri Leith 'twas a faultless arrangement,*
> *They were burned by Manannan.*

At that time there was a new king of all Ireland, and his name was Eochaid Airem, perhaps descended from the original Eochaid, or simply having taken his name. All five parts of Ireland submitted to him, each with its own king. He commanded them to attend a great festival at Tara, so that he could decide their taxes and tributes, but they refused to attend, for he had no queen – and what was a king in those days without a queen?

So High King Eochaid sent forth his envoys to every part of the country, looking for the fairest maiden that could be found, and a maiden she had to be, for he declared that no other man should have known her before him. Each of the envoys returned with a maiden, but fairest of them all was Etain daughter of Etar, and Eochaid married her, for she was his match in beauty and form and lineage, in splendour and youth and fame.

But what happened next was a surprise to everyone! His brother, whose name was Ailill Anguba, was sorely struck and overcome by Etain's ethereal, ancient beauty, and oftentimes would gaze at her furtively over his cups. He was deeply ashamed but could not hide from his feelings, for desire is stronger than character.

He kept these feelings to himself, and he sickened as a result, a man at war with himself, and so sick he became that he came close to death. Fachtna, the High king's healer, came to him and gave this diagnosis:

"One of the two pains you have that kill man and no physician can heal, the pain of love and the pain of jealousy."

And yet still Ailill Anguba did not confess the cause of his ailment. As he lay dying in his Dún, Eochaid went on a tour of his dominion, leaving Etain alone with him to oversee his grave-digging, his lamentations and his cattle-slaughter.

Each day she came to him for conversation, and each day his sickness lifted little by little, which was noticed by Etain. She asked him the cause of his sickness, and he declared at last his love.

"Pity that you have been so long without telling it," said she, "had we but known you should have been healed a while ago."

"Even this day I shall be whole again if you are willing," said Ailill Anguba.

"I am willing indeed," she said.

And she came to him every day as he lay sick to bathe his head and carve his meat, and to pour water on his hands. When thrice nine days had passed, Ailill Anguba was fit as a fiddle, and he asked her:

"When shall I have from you what is still lacking to cure me?"

"You shall have it tomorrow," said she, "but not in the prince's dwelling shall he be put to shame. Come to me tomorrow on the hill above the court."

Well I can tell you that Ailill Anguba watched through the night, but when the hour came for his tryst, he fell fast asleep, and didn't wake until the next day.

Etain went to meet him, and found instead a man who looked very like him, who said he could go no further due to his weakness and sickness, so she returned home.

The next day Ailill Anguba awoke and there was much confusion between them, for he had no memory of any tryst, and felt it was his sickness muddling his mind. But Etain was sympathetic, and said they could meet again that very night, so he built a huge fire and kept a bucket of water by his side to wash his eyes, in order that he should stay awake.

But again he fell fast asleep, and three times more this same thing happened, until on the fourth tryst, Etain challenged the man who met her for their romantic encounter.

"Tis not with you that I have trusted," said she, "who are you that have come to meet me? The man with whom I have made a tryst, 'tis not for sin or hurt that the tryst has been made with him, but that one fit to be king of Ireland might be saved from the sickness that has fallen upon him."

The figure in the shape of Ailill Anguba ceased his moaning and griping and looked at her with clear eyes, saying

"It is more fitting for you to come to me, for you were Etain Echraide, daughter of Ailill, and I was your husband. I have paid your huge bride price in the great plains and rivers of Ireland, and have left in place of you your weight of gold and silver."

"Who are you?" she asked.

"No hard matter," he responded, "for I am called Midir! It was the sorcery of Fuamnach and the spells of Bresal Etarlam that separated us. Will you come with me now?"

"I will not," she said "for I am the wife of the High King of Ireland – will I trade that for the company of a man I don't know?"

"It was I," said Midir, "that put love for you into Ailill's mind, so that his flesh and blood fell away from him. And it was I that took from him all carnal desire, so that your honour might not suffer. But come to my land with me if Eochaid bids you."

"Willingly," said Etain, and returned to her house, where she found Ailill Anguba cured of both his sickness and his lust, and soon the High King returned with rejoicing for the good outcome.

Later that summer, and a lovely summer it was, warm and fulsome, Eochaid Airem, the High King of all Ireland, from his slumber and went to the terrace to gaze upon the radiant colourful plains of his realm. He paused in surprise though, for standing before him on the terrace was a strange warrior!

Clad in a purple tunic, with golden hair bound by a golden band, of shining blue eyes and carrying a five pointed spear behind a gem-studded white shield, he was an unexpected guest, since the courts had not yet been opened and Eochaid had not seen him in Tara the previous night.

Calling out a challenge, he asked the fair warrior what his name was.

"Not famous," said he, "I am Midir."

"And what brings you to my court?" asked Eochaid.

"Why, I seek to play fidchell with you, oh High King!" replied the warrior.

"In truth I'm good at fidchell," said Eochaid, "but the queen is asleep, and my fidchell board is in her house!"

"I have here," said Midir, "a fidchell board that is not inferior," which was true, he had a silver board and golden men, and each corner was lit up by precious stones, with a bag for the men made of plaited links of bronze.

Midir set up the board, but Eochaid held up his hand.

"I will only play for a stake," he said.

"And what shall that be?" asked Midir.

"It's all the same to me," replied Eochaid.

"If you win," said Midir, "you'll have from me fifty dark grey steeds with dappled blood-red heads, pointed-ears, broad-chested, with distended nostrils, slender limbs, mighty, keen eyes, huge, swift, steady easily yoked, with fifty enamelled reins. They shall be here at the fifth hour tomorrow, if you are agreeable."

Indeed Eochaid was amenable, and agreed to pay the same if he lost. So they played, and Midir lost, then took his board and himself away, although Eochaid didn't know how he was coming or going.

The next morning the agreed-upon stake arrived, and Midir popped up beside the High King, who to his credit didn't jump or even blink.

"What is promised is due," said Midir, "would you care for another game?"

"Willingly," said Eochaid, "but only for a stake!"

"If you win," said Midir, "you'll have from me fifty young boars, curly-mottled, grey-bellied, blue-backed, with horses hooves to them, together with a vat of blackthorn into which they all will fit. Further, fifty gold-hilted swords, and again fifty red-eared cows with white red-eared calves with a bronze spancel on each calf. Further, fifty grey wethers with red heads, three-headed, three-horned. Further, fifty ivory-hilted swords. Further, fifty speckled cloaks, but each fifty of them on its own day."

Overhearing this conversation, Eochaid's foster father took him aside and asked where Midir had come from with all this wealth.

"You must be careful of him, and get the best use from him," Eochaid's foster father warned, "it is a man of magic power that has come to you, my son, to lay heavy burdens on him."

And in the Mitchell games that followed, High King Eochaid laid upon Midir famous tasks, to clear Meath of stone, to put rushes over Tethba, a causeway over My Marriage, and a wood over Breifne, of which the poets write:

> *These are the four things*
> *that Eochaid Airem imposed*
> *on many a manly-visaged throng*
> *with many a shield and spear:*

> *A causeway over Moin Marriage,*
> *a wood over Breifne, without difficulty,*
> *a clearing of stone from the hillocks of great Meath,*
> *and rushes over Tethba.*

"But this is too much, and too hard!" said Midir.

"These are the stakes," said Eochaid implacably.

"Then if you win," said Midir, "grant me one request – as much as you can prevent it, let no man or woman step outside their own door until dawn tomorrow."

Eochaid agreed, but told his steward to set a watch on the causeway, to see how this great feat was to be achieved. He reported that it seemed to him as though all the men in the world had come to the bog. They piled their clothes into a great hill, and Midir went up and stood on the top, urging on the host on every side. From the sound of it, you'd think everyone on earth was shouting!

Next, clay and gravel and stones were placed upon the bog, not by the foreheads of oxen as the men of Ireland were used to doing, but rather by the backs and arms of the people of the mounds! Whole trees and trunks they laid as the foundation of the causeway, and there would be no better causeway except the High King had disobeyed Midir and left a watcher, so there were some defects in the work. As the Steward told it, there was no magic power to surpass what he had seen.

As they talked, they spotted Midir approaching, and him looking warlike and with an evil glint in his eye. They were afraid to see him coming, as well they might be, but Eochaid greeted him nonetheless.

"Fierce and unreasonable was the burden you laid upon me," said Midir, "and now I'm angry at you!"

"I am not angry at you," said Eochaid, "perhaps, to set your mind at ease, we can play another game of Fidchell?"

"Agreed," said Midir, "and the stake shall be one wish from either of us," and that day Eochaid lost the game. Eochaid stayed calm, but asked Midir what he would have for his wish.

"My arms around Etain and a kiss from her," said Midir.

Eochaid was silent for a while, then said "Come a month from today and that shall be given to you."

And Midir recalled the soft song he had sung to Etain the year before:

> O Fair Lady, wilt you come with me
> to the wondrous land wherein harmony is,
> hair is like the crown of the primrose there.
> and the body is smooth and white as snow.
>
> There, is neither mine nor thine,
> white are teeth there, dark brows.
> A delight of the eye the number of our hosts,
> every cheek there is of the hue of the foxglove.
>
> A gillyflower is each one's neck,
> A delight of the eye are blackbirds' eggs.
> Though the prospect of Mag Fail,
> 'tis desolate after frequenting Mag Mar.

Though choice you deem the ale of Inis Fail,
More intoxicating is the ale of Tir Mar.
A wondrous land is the land I tell of;
youth departs not before old.

Warm sweet streams flow through the land,
the choice of mead and wine.
Stately folk without blemish,
conception without sin, without lust.

We see everyone on every side,
and no one sees us.
It is the darkness of Adam's transgression
that hath prevented us from being counted.

O woman, if you come to my proud folk,
a crown of gold shall be upon your head
honey, wine, ale, fresh milk, and drink,
you shall have with me there, O Fair Lady.

And what happened next was written in the book of Druim Sneachta. In readiness for the visit from Midir, Eochaid the High King mustered the flower of the warriors of Ireland to Tara, and the very best of the war bands, then he arranged them in circles around his stronghold, and manned every wall and door with a fell-handed warrior.

The king and queen sat in the middle of the house with the doors locked, knowing well a mighty magician was on the way. Etain was serving the lords on that night, for the serving of drink was a special gift of hers.

And sure enough who did they see coming at the midnight hour but Midir, walking into the courtroom of Tara as bold as brass! Always a handsome fellow, that night he was even fairer. Everyone was astonished and silence held sway, but Eochaid gulped and made him welcome.

"I have come for what has been pledged to me," said Midir, "let it be given to me. What is promised is due. What was promised, I have given you."

"I hadn't thought about it," said Eochaid, although in truth he had thought about it a great deal.

"Etain herself promised me that she would come away with me," said Midir, causing Etain to blush.

"Do not blush, Etain," said Midir, "it is not unfaithful of you. I have been a year," said he, "seeking you with gifts and treasures, the most beautiful in Ireland, nor do I take you without Eochaid's leave. Did you think all these things happened by chance?"

"I told you," she said, "I will not go to you unless Eochaid yields me, and if he does, you may take me."

"I will not sell my wife," said Eochaid, "but if Midir wishes to put his arms around Etain in the middle of the house, as you are, that is fine."

And with that Midir approached the lady, putting his weapons in his left hand and his right arm around her, he kissed her and with a whoosh, they disappeared up the chimney hole, and those watching outside swore they saw two swans soaring away from Tara!

Eochaid and his warriors were shocked and ashamed, and set out upon the instant to chase after them, stopping to rest in many places, such as the fabled Oweynagat.

Across fairy mound after fairy mound, sidh after sidh, they followed in warlike fashion, bringing with them mighty oxen and many men of broad back, digging up each mound as they went. Eochaid was filled with a terrible rage at the treachery done to him, and he was determined to dig up every sidh in the country if that's what it took to find his wife. And truly, the might of a High king was to be feared, even by the sidhe.

When they began digging at Sidh Barn Find, one of those inside came out and told them the woman was not there, but instead they should go to the home of the king of the Sidhe mounds, to the north, and dig there instead.

They reached this mighty mound and began their digging, but they were a year and three months at it, getting nowhere, what they dug up one day would be restored the next morning!

In frustration Eochaid decided a trick had been played on him, so he went right back to Sidh Ban Find and began digging again. One of those within came out to appeal his vandalism.

"What have you against us, O Eochaid?" they asked, "We have not taken your wife. No injury has been done to you by us."

"I will not leave," said he, "until you tell me how I might get my wife from that magical mound!"

"Take blind whelps with you," he was told, "and blind cats, and set them loose after and before you work, each and every day."

Thus instructed, he returned to the home of Midir, Sidh Bri Leith, and set to work with vigour and vengeance in their eyes, and this time their efforts paid off! As they were razing the mound, who should come out but Midir himself.

"What do you have against me," asked Midir, "you did me wrong, and have put great troubles on me – as well as selling your wife to me! Do me no more injury."

"She will not be with you," said Eochaid firmly.

"As you wish," said Midir, "she shall not. Your wife will come to you at the third hour tomorrow, so leave me if that suits you well enough!"

Eochaid accepted and returned home after having bound the covenant, but on the third hour of the next day, what did he see but fifty women who looked alike and dressed alike to Etain! All of his armies and hosts were silent, looking in confusion on the scene, but they were tired from this lengthy adventure, and bid him take his wife.

"What do you think?" asked Eochaid of the men of Ireland.

"We have no resolve in this," they said.

"I do," said Eochaid, "for my wife is the best at serving drinks in Ireland."

So they divided up the women and divided them up again and again until there were only two remaining. Eochaid gazed upon them in puzzlement, for one was Etain, but had not her trick of serving drinks. They all took counsel and said

"This is Etain, but it is not Etain, at least, not her serving," so they settled on that one as the wife of Eochaid and everyone departed, the women included. Eochaid's war upon the King of the Mounds became a matter of great legend, and they spoke with satisfaction of the high feats done by the oxen, and their rescue of a woman from the mounds.

Well, the next summer, and a fine warm summer it was, Eochaid arose from his bed and was holding a conversation with his queen in the court, asking who should walk in but Midir! They greeted one another with caution.

"You have not played me fair with the hardships you inflicted on me, considering the power you have and still demanded all that from me. There was nothing you didn't ask of me," said Midir.

"I didn't sell you my wife," said Eochaid.

"Answer me this then," said Midir, "is your conscience clear and your mind at ease as far as we go?"

"It is," said Eochaid.

"As is mine," chuckled Midir, "for your wife was pregnant when she was taken from you, and she bore a daughter, and it is she who is with you. Your wife, meanwhile, is with me, and you let her go a second time!" and with that he vanished in his way.

Eochaid dared not to dig another mound, for the covenant he had agreed with Midir forbade it, and he was greatly and terribly grieved that he had lain with his own daughter. He learned that she was with the child, and told his men to throw the child into a pit of beasts, so that they might never look upon one another.

They took the child to the house of Findlam the herdsman of Tara and threw the child in with the dogs, but the herdsman and his wife returned to find the creatures nestled up beside the babe. They were amazed, for they were without a child, and so they raised her as their own, and she grew strong and a master of many arts and crafts.

After that Eochaid Airem grew darker and more of an evil nature, and his mind was troubled. He laid hard tribute and steep taxes on the five parts of Ireland, until at least the people could take no more, and a plot was hatched against Eochaid. His house was burned and his head was taken and brought to Connachta, and this poem was written of his end:

> *Eochaid Airem, noble, fair and graceful,*
> *eminent high-king of Ireland,*
> *extended his bold hard tribute,*
> *it spread through Banda off of the brown cloaks.*
>
> *The folk of Tethba stubbornly fights*
> *got the tribute of the king of Ireland.*
> *The lawgiving king who ruled them, put*
> *the seventh (part) on them alone.*
>
> *Heavy sorrow of the host came*
> *because of the monstrous unjust law,*
> *anger was kindled because of it,*
> *until Eochaid Airem was slain.*
>
> *The folk of Tethba, mighty of yore,*
> *slew Eochaid of Fremaind*
> *'Twas not strength with cause on their part,*
> *because of the monstrous unjust law.*
>
> *Morel was the name of the king at first*
> *by whom the great deed was done,*
> *Fir Chul the name of the men of Tethba in the east*
> *when Dun Freimann was overpowered.*
>
> *Though 'tis said that Signal of the spears*
> *slew Eochaid Airem,*

he died himself before Eochaid of Fremaind
in the succession of leaders.

Sigmall of the battling spears died
by the smooth bright face of Manannan;
avast long time in the east, without weakness,
before Eochaid met his death.

The two Signals of Sid Nennta,
intrepid their feet, mighty their prowess,
Small son of Coirpre of the battles,
Sigmall who was at Eochaid's death.

Small son of Brestine of lasting memory,
king of Bentraige with great triumph,
and great Mormael from the Plain,
by them, Eochaid perished.

Mysticism and Magic

I See The Moon The Moon Sees Me.

Our Irish ancestors from olden times were fascinated with the sky and its inhabitants, how they moved, what they meant and where their celestial lives intersected with our own. The Tuatha Dé Danann loved the sun foremost but others built places aligned to the movements of the moon and stars, many of which predate the solar structures.

There is even evidence for a struggle that took place between the two belief systems as waves of invasions ebbed and flowed, drowning the sorrowing soil of Ireland with the blood of heroes, but despite being driven deep, we can still hear echoes of that long-gone time if we listen to the land closely enough.

Nature was seen to move in cycles, and it was thought that the rebirth of the new moon signalled the beginning of these little seasons. On the night of the new moon, if one were to borrow a piece of silver it would turn to two by the end of the month, and if a person was to turn the coins in their pockets on that same night, they would prosper greatly.

"Whatever you have in your hand when you see the new moon first, you will have plenty of that before the next new moon comes."

The mystery of the changing moon was near to the heart of old druidry, and they even laid out their calendars following its shifting nature. Best known of these is the Coligny calendar, made up of bronze fragments which were once a single huge plate. Each year was divided into thirteen months.

Such was their reverence for the moon that they would rarely refer to it directly, instead using words like "gealach" which means brightness. This also hints at the uses to which they put hawthorn, or the sceach gheal – moon thorn. "Gealach na gcoinnlíní" is the Harvest Moon, where coinnlíní is the Irish for a stubble field with stalks left after reaping. "Seán na Gealaí" is Jack of the Lantern, "corrán gealaí" is a crescent moon.

Those touched by the moon were considered le gealaí, or keeping company with the moon. Some believed that sleeping directly under the moonlight would lead to bad dreams and ill temper, or at worst, blindness, paralysis and other afflictions.

Lunar eclipses were times of importance to the ancient Gaels and were associated with the rabbit and the hare, both symbols of fertility.

They may also have had a "festival of light" to welcome eclipses, which the druids could predict.

Long before the druids or even the working of metal was known in Ireland, the people of Ireland had great knowledge of the moon and stars, as can be seen in the great passage mound of Knowth which is only a short distance from Newgrange.

There is a wealth of lunar symbolism on the many engravings in Knowth, and the eighteen monuments around the central mound, are both far older than Knowth and echo the lunar cycle, which takes eighteen years to complete.

Some researchers believe that many of the kerbstones at Knowth functioned as calendars for counting and marking lunar cycles. At certain regular intervals in the ancient past, at least twice if not four or eight times during the eighteen-year lunar cycle, the east and west chambers of Knowth were lit by both the sun and moon simultaneously.

If the light of the moon shone onto the back stone in one of these passages, it would light up what some believe to be one of the oldest maps of the lunar landscape in the world. Several other stones appear to depict phases of the moon, perhaps as a calendar of the future or a memorial of past events of importance.

At Dowth, there are one hundred and fifteen kerb stones, exactly half the number of lunar months in a "moon swing" cycle, the time it takes the moon to run through its extreme rising and setting points on the horizon and back again. The mythology surrounding the building of Dowth tells us that the men working to construct a mound so their king Bresail Bó-Dibad could reach the heavens abandoned their work halfway through when the sun fell into darkness, or an eclipse took place.

The ancient Greek Diodorus Siculus wrote of the '" Island of the Hyperboreans" in and around the first century BC

"There is also on the island both a magnificent sacred precinct of Apollo and a notable temple which is adorned with many votive offerings and is spherical in shape... They say also that the moon, as viewed from this island, appears to be but a little distance from the Earth and to have upon it prominences, like those of the Earth, which are visible to the eye. The account is also given that the god visits the island every nineteen years."

Since these ancient mounds were decorated with glittering white quartz pieces, some have suggested they were meant to represent or reflect the moon.

The cairn in Carrowkeel in county Sligo also seems to have been built to observe the longer lunar cycles.

Some parts of the Beaghmore stone circles are astronomically linked with dawn and dusk on the solstices, but unusually, for the most part, the overall alignment is more closely connected to the phases of the moon. This forms part of a different and perhaps older tradition than the cross-quarter celebrations.

Nighttime is truly magical amid the Beaghmore stones, due to the remoteness and altitude of the site, the sky is darker here than almost anywhere else in the country, and it was under silverine moonlight that rituals were conducted here of old. The purpose of these rites is not known today, but the seventh circle might give some hint, the one known as the Dragon's Teeth.

For within the eight hundred stones of this seventh circle, seven being a number associated with the lunar cycle, were discovered the remains of several children of great antiquity, and some visitors have reported hearing the voices of children, or even the touch of children's hand on their own as they made a hasty departure!

One of the highest figures among the ancestors the Gaels reverenced was Elatha, Ealadha or Elathan, a prince of the Fomorians and the father of Bres of the Tuatha Dé Danann. He was most associated with the moon since he visited Eriú by night in a silver boat.

Seeds planted and roof thatching begun when the moon was young would be smiled upon, and children born on this night were considered favoured. Animals were slaughtered during this time so that they would "swell in the boil". Hair should also be cut when the moon is waxing to ensure subsequent growth, although other traditions hold that hair should only be cut during the waning phases so that it might be longer before needing your next haircut!

Contrariwise, the fading moon was thought to take disease and sores along with it.

Catching the first glimpse of a new moon through glass was to suffer bad luck for the coming month, and worse yet if you happened to see it over your left shoulder! Whereas seeing it over the right shoulder was fine, similar to walking diesel or clockwise around ancient stones when seeking a blessing.

Should the moon pop out in front of you however you were due for a fall. There must have been some strange dances taking place on that night! This might be why on a bright moonlit night the fairies were said to be out singing and dancing.

Here we can also see the admixture of old pagan beliefs with Christianity, in the veneration of the new moon for protection as long as it lived. A seventeenth-century German writer wrote: "The wild Irish have this custom, that when the moon is new they squat upon their knees and pray to the moon that it may leave them vigorous and healthy."

Petitioners would kneel before the moon, say a Pater Noster or Ave Maria, make the sign of the cross or other pious motion and then sing out:

"Oh Moon! May thou leave us safe, as thou hast found us!"

or alternatively

*"God and the holy Virgin be about me!
I see the moon, and the moon sees me
God bless the moon, and God bless me!"*

When the new moon first appeared, people would bless themselves and say "Go mbeí mis seo and tam seo arís" and wish for something, and it might just come true.

The eternal return of the moon was naturally something mysterious, there was a saying about the new moon: "On the first night nobody sees it, on the second night the birds see it, and on the third night everybody sees it."

People used to say that the potatoes were not ripe to dig until the first harvest moon's full. And if that came late, the potatoes would be poor eating. The harvest moon was said to gather the cabbage. While the moon was filling it was a good time for fishing but while it was going back you would hardly catch any fish at all.

The motions of the moon were used by the people of Ireland to predict their futures, if the new moon was on its back that was a sure sign of rain but if it stood upright that was a sign of fine weather. If the new moon was pale with a ring around it, "súil circe ré" or the moon of the hen's eye, that was a sign of rain.

If you were working when you saw the new moon you would be at that work for a long time. If the new moon appeared early in the sky, rain would follow after, but if the new moon was red, the wind would chase hard on its heels.

It was often held that a full moon on Saturday was a sign of bad weather or some other local misfortune.

Young Irish women seeking a sign of their future husbands appealed to the new moon as well, kneeling and taking a black-handled knife before lifting a sod of turf from under their right knee and from under the toe of their right foot, calling out the following cant:

*"New moon, new moon,
Happy may I be
Whoever is my true love
This night may I see."*

And many a young Irish couple walked hand in hand under the waxing moon.

Printed in Great Britain
by Amazon